Disclaimer

The following spell book is designed to provide information and guidance on the practice of Wicca. However, it is important to note that Wicca is a spiritual practice that requires a deep understanding of its principles and practices.

This spell book is not intended to replace or substitute for professional medical, legal, or financial advice. If you are experiencing physical or mental health problems, legal issues, or financial difficulties, we strongly recommend seeking the advice of a licensed professional.

The spells and rituals included in this spell book are intended for educational and entertainment purposes only. They are not guaranteed to produce specific results and should not be relied upon as a substitute for professional medical or psychological treatment.

It is important to use caution when practicing any form of spellcraft, as there is always a risk of unintended consequences.

We cannot be held responsible for any negative effects that may result from the use of the spells and rituals in this book.

Additionally, it is important to note that Wicca is a personal spiritual practice, and each individual's experiences and beliefs may vary. The spells and rituals included in this book are designed as guidelines and suggestions, but it is ultimately up to the individual to decide what resonates with them and what does not.

By using this spell book, you acknowledge that you are doing so at your own risk and that you assume full responsibility for any consequences that may result from its use. We do not guarantee the accuracy, reliability, or completeness of the information contained in this spell book, and we cannot be held responsible for any errors or omissions.

CONTENTS

CONTENTS

Introduction

Wicca magic is a beautiful and ancient practice that draws its roots from pre-Christian, pagan religions. It is a form of witchcraft that focuses on working with the natural world and harnessing the power of the elements to create positive change in one's life. Wiccans believe that everything in the universe is interconnected, and that by tapping into this interconnectedness, they can bring about positive changes in themselves and the world around them.

But Wicca magic is much more than just casting spells. It is a way of life that encourages practitioners to live in harmony with the natural world and with each other. Wiccans believe in the concept of "harm none," which means that they strive to avoid causing harm to anyone, including themselves, animals, and the environment. They also believe in the power of community, and often gather together for rituals and celebrations.

Wicca also emphasizes the importance of ethical considerations in magic and spell-casting. Many Wiccans follow the Wiccan Rede, which states, "An it harm none, do what ye will." This means that Wiccans should only use magic for positive and benevolent purposes and should avoid using magic to harm others. Wiccans also believe in the concept of threefold law, which states that whatever energy you put out into the universe will be returned to you threefold.

OPULENCE EVOCATIONS

MONEY MAGNET SPELL

The origins of the Money Magnet Spell are unclear, but it is thought to have been passed down through generations of Wiccans and practitioners of magic. Some believe that merchants and traders originally used it to attract prosperity and success to their businesses, while others say that it was created by witches to help bring financial stability to their communities.

Over time, the Money Magnet Spell has evolved to include various ingredients and incantations that are thought to enhance its power. Some Wiccans believe that the spell must be performed during specific phases of the moon, such as the full moon, to maximize its effectiveness. Others believe that it should be performed during astrological events related to abundance, such as when Jupiter is in a favorable position.

Despite its popularity, the Money Magnet Spell is a controversial spell in Wiccan circles. Some Wiccans believe that it is unethical to use magic for personal gain, while others believe that it is a perfectly acceptable use of magic.
Regardless of personal beliefs, the Money Magnet Spell remains a popular spell in Wiccan magic and is used by many to attract abundance and financial stability into their lives.

You will need the following:

- A green candle
- Bay leaves
- Cinnamon sticks
- Ginger root
- Nutmeg
- Thyme
- A piece of paper and pen
- A green cloth

To perform the spell, follow these steps:

1. Clean and bless your working space.
2. Place the green candle on your altar.
3. Light the green candle and call upon the spirit of Abundance and Prosperity.
4. Write down the amount of money you want to attract on the piece of paper.
5. Mix the bay leaves, cinnamon sticks, ginger root, nutmeg, and thyme together.
6. Sprinkle the mixture around the green candle.
7. Fold the piece of paper with your intention written on it and place it in front of the green candle.
8. Wrap the green cloth around the candle and the piece of paper.
9. Repeat the following incantation three times:
   "O powers of abundance, hear my plea. Bring wealth, prosperity, and abundance to me. Money and riches flow my way, Bringing abundance to me day by day. With this spell, I call upon the gods, To fill my life with bountiful odds. Prosperity, abundance, and wealth untold May mote it be, with this incantation told.
10. Let the candle burn down completely.
11. Store the green cloth and the remaining herbs in a safe place.

ABUNDANCE JAR SPELL

The Abundance Jar Spell is a spell in Wiccan magic that is used to attract abundance and prosperity into one's life.

The origins of the Abundance Jar Spell can be traced back to ancient cultures, such as the Egyptians, who believed that the accumulation of wealth was a sign of blessings from the gods. They would create offerings to the gods and bury them in jars, hoping to attract prosperity and abundance into their lives.

In Wicca, the spell is seen as a way to connect with the energies of the earth and the divine and to ask for help in attracting abundance and prosperity into one's life. The spell is often performed during the full moon when the energies of the moon are said to be at their strongest and most conducive to manifestation.

Over time, the spell has evolved and adapted, with different practitioners adding their own unique twists and interpretations. Some Wiccans add spells or affirmations to their Abundance Jars, while others simply fill them with symbols of abundance and let the spell work on its own.

You will need the following:

- A clear glass jar with a lid
- Green candles
- A green cloth
- Coins or money

- Basil leaves
- Cinnamon sticks
- Orange slices
- Cloves
- A pen

To perform the spell, follow these steps:

1. Cleanse your jar, candles, and other ingredients by smudging them with sage or using holy water.
2. Wrap the jar with the green cloth and place the green candles on either side of the jar.
3. Light the candles and let them burn for a few minutes.
4. Add the coins or money to the jar, along with the basil leaves, cinnamon sticks, orange slices, and cloves.
5. Close the jar and hold it in your hands.
6. Visualize your life filled with abundance and prosperity.
7. Repeat the following incantation three times:

   "Oh powerful spirits of abundance and prosperity, I call upon you to hear my plea. Bring forth the blessings of wealth and success, Infinite and never-ending, I confess. By the power of the elements, earth, air, fire, and sea, I invite you to flow freely into me. So mote it be, so mote it be, with harm to none, this spell shall be."

8. Place the jar in a safe place, such as a shelf or table, where it will not be disturbed.
9. Leave the candles to burn out completely.

MONEY DRAWING SPELL

The Money Drawing Spell with Sage is a Wiccan spell used to attract wealth and financial abundance. This spell involves the use of sage to purify and protect, as well as other symbols and materials associated with wealth and prosperity.

Sage is often used in money spells because it is believed to cleanse the space of negative energy and to create a positive and receptive environment for attracting wealth and prosperity. The act of smudging with sage is seen as a way to purify the aura and to align one's energy with the energy of abundance. The smoke from the sage is believed to carry the spell and incantation to the universe, where it can be acted upon to bring forth desired results.

You will need the following:

- Sage bundle or loose sage leaves
- A fireproof bowl or container
- A lighter or matches
- Green candles
- Coins or other symbols of wealth (such as a money tree, a piggy bank, etc.)
- A piece of paper and pen

To perform the spell, follow these steps:

1. Choose a place where you can perform the spell undisturbed. Light the sage bundle or loose sage leaves using a lighter or matches and hold it over the fireproof container to catch any ashes.
2. Once the sage starts to smoke, use your hand or a feather to fan the smoke into the air. You can also use a fan made specifically for smudging.
3. Begin to walk around the room, making sure to get the smoke into all the nooks and crannies. As you do this, you can recite the following incantation or one of your own:
4. "By the power of the elements of air and fire, I purify this space of all negativity and desire. With the smoke of sage, I dispel all fear, Bringing forth abundance, joy, and good cheer.
5. Let the smoke rise, carrying with it my intention, To attract wealth and prosperity without any retention. Let my mind, body, and soul be cleansed and clear, So that abundance may freely flow, drawing near.
6. With this sage, I banish all doubts and worry, Making room for abundance to flourish in a hurry. Let my home, my life, and my finances be blessed, With prosperity and abundance, that shall never rest."
7. Place the green candles on a table or altar and light them.
8. Place the coins or other symbols of wealth on the table or altar.
9. Please write down the amount of money you would like to attract on a piece of paper and place it next to the candles and symbols of wealth.
10. Close your eyes and visualize yourself having the money you have written down. See yourself using it to pay bills, buy things you need, and save for the future.
11. Repeat the following incantation three times:

"Money, money, hear my call. Bring abundance and prosperity to my hall. By the power of the elements of earth and air, I invite wealth and abundance without a single care.
Let my finances now be repaired, With an influx of wealth that I have declared. I call upon the forces of nature and magic, To bring forth abundance and let my finances be fantastic.
Money, money, flow to me, In abundance and prosperity, endlessly.
By the power of sage, I ask thee, To grant my wish and bring prosperity.
So mote it be."

12. Extinguish the sage by blowing it out or placing it in the fireproof container to allow it to burn out on its own.
13. Allow the green candles to burn out on their own.

GOLD RIBBON SPELL

The Gold Ribbon Spell is a ritual in Wicca to attract wealth and prosperity. This spell involves tying a gold ribbon around a piece of money or a talisman that represents your financial goals and using visualization and affirmations to focus your intention and harness the energies of the universe.

The power of the Gold Ribbon Spell lies in its ability to combine the energy of the universe with the intention and visualization of the practitioner. By tying the gold ribbon around a piece of money or talisman and focusing on an affirmation, the practitioner is able to tap into the powerful energy of the universe and bring abundance and prosperity into their life.

In the tradition of Wicca, the Gold Ribbon Spell is often performed during a full moon, when the energy of the moon is believed to be at its peak. The spell is also commonly performed during the celebration of Imbolc, a festival that marks the beginning of spring and symbolizes the return of abundance and prosperity after the long, dark winter.

You will need the following:

- a piece of gold ribbon
- a piece of money or a talisman that represents your financial goals

To perform the spell, follow these steps:

1. Make sure you are in a quiet place where you can focus on your intention.
2. Choose an affirmation: Before you begin the spell, you will need to choose an affirmation. This can be something as simple as "I am worthy of wealth and prosperity" or "Money flows effortlessly into my life."
3. Tie the gold ribbon: Take the gold ribbon and tie it around the piece of money or talisman. As you do this, focus on your affirmation, and feel the energy of the universe aligning with your intention.
4. Visualize your goals: Close your eyes and visualize yourself as already having achieved your financial goals. See yourself living the life you desire, surrounded by abundance and prosperity. Hold this visualization in your mind for several minutes, feeling the emotions of joy and gratitude.
5. Speak your affirmation: Once you have visualized your goals, you can seal the spell by speaking your affirmation several times. This will help to solidify your intention and focus your energy on attracting wealth and prosperity.
6. Speak these words as you tie the gold ribbon around the piece of money or talisman and as you focus on your affirmation and visualization. You can also speak the incantation several times to seal the spell and reinforce your intention:

"Ribbon of gold, the symbol of wealth, Bring to me abundance and prosperity, By the power of the universe, I call forth financial success, With this spell, I seal my intention, And let it be done, so mote it be."

7. Carry the talisman with you: You can now carry the piece of money or talisman with you or place it in a place where you will see it often, such as your wallet or near your financial documents. This will help to keep your intention and energy focused on your financial goals.

8. Practice positive affirmations: Throughout the day, repeat your affirmation and focus on positive thoughts about your financial situation. This will help to strengthen the energies you have summoned and bring abundance and prosperity into your life.

WEALTH OIL SPELL

Wealth Oil Spell is a type of ritual oil used in Wiccan magic to attract wealth, abundance, and prosperity into one's life. This spell can be used to anoint candles, crystals, talismans, money, or other objects to empower them with the energy of abundance and draw financial success toward you.

The use of oils for wealth and prosperity specifically can be traced back to medieval Europe, where merchants and wealthy individuals would anoint their coins and other financial documents with special oils to protect and attract wealth. This practice was later adopted by Wiccans and other practitioners of magic, who incorporated it into their own rituals and spells.

Aside from using the oil to anoint objects, the Wealth Oil Spell can also be used in other ways to enhance its potency. For example, you can use the oil to anoint yourself by massaging it into your skin, focusing on your intentions as you do so. You can also use the oil to create a prosperity sachet by placing it in a small cloth bag and carrying it with you or placing it near your financial documents.

You will need the following:

- Base oil (such as olive oil)
- A pinch of cinnamon
- A pinch of basil
- A pinch of nutmeg
- A pinch of allspice

- A small piece of rose quartz (optional)

To perform the spell, follow these steps:

1. Start by cleansing your workspace and your ingredients. You can do this by smudging the area with sage smoke or by visualizing a bright, white light surrounding everything and purifying it of negative energy.
2. In a small container, mix the base oil with the cinnamon, basil, nutmeg, and allspice. Stir the ingredients together with a wooden spoon.
3. Hold the rose quartz in your dominant hand and visualize yourself surrounded by abundance and prosperity. See yourself with an overflowing bank account, a fulfilling job, and plenty of material possessions. Repeat the following affirmations:

   "I am worthy of wealth and abundance. Money flows freely into my life. I am open to receiving abundance in all forms."

4. Place the rose quartz in the container with the oil mixture and continue to stir while focusing on your intentions of abundance and prosperity.
5. When you feel that the oil is charged with your energy and intentions, you can use it to anoint candles, crystals, money, or any other object that you would like to empower with the energy of wealth. To do this, simply dip your finger into the oil and trace symbols or words related to abundance and prosperity onto the object.

WEALTHY WAY SPELL

The Wealthy Way Spell is a Wiccan spell for attracting prosperity and abundance into your life. It is a manifestation spell that calls upon the energies of the earth and the sky to attract wealth and abundance into one's life. By walking through a park or forest and collecting natural items, the practitioner creates a sacred space to focus their energy and intention on their desired outcome. The use of a green candle, which is associated with growth and abundance, and the recitation of an incantation, serves to amplify the practitioner's intention and bring their desires into reality.

You will need the following:

- leaves, flowers, and other natural items
- green candle
- one cloth

To perform the spell, follow these steps:

1. Preparation: Choose a day when you have time to take a leisurely walk in a park or forest. Dress in comfortable clothing and bring a small bag to collect items that you find along the way.
2. Take a Walk: As you walk, pay attention to the natural items that catch your eye. You can pick up leaves, flowers, stones, or any other items that feel significant to you. You can also stop to meditate and focus on your intention for abundance.
3. Create a Sacred Space: Once you have collected a few items, find a quiet place where you can create a sacred space. You can lay out a cloth, light candles, and create a circle with your collected items.

4. Focus on Your Intention: Light a green candle and hold it in front of you. Focus on your intention for wealth and prosperity, and visualize yourself surrounded by abundance and financial stability. Repeat the following incantation:

5. "Wealthy way, I call upon thee. Bring abundance and prosperity to me. With the power of the earth and the sky, I invite wealth and abundance, by and by So mote it be."

6. Close the Circle: When you feel that you have connected with the energies of prosperity and abundance, blow out the candle, and close the circle. Thank the elements and the universe for their support.

7. Use Your Intentions: After the spell, carry the items you collected with you or place them in a prominent place to remind you of your intention for wealth and prosperity. Continue to focus on your intention and visualize yourself surrounded by abundance and financial stability.

LUNAR ABUNDANCE SPELL

The Lunar Abundance Spell is a Wiccan spell for attracting prosperity and abundance into your life using the energies of the moon. The spell is performed during a full moon, when the moon is at its strongest and most potent, to harness its powerful energies for manifestation.

In the Wiccan tradition, the full moon is associated with abundance and prosperity, as well as with the goddesses of fertility and growth. During the full moon, Wiccans would gather to perform spells and rituals to invoke the energies of abundance and to ask for blessings from the goddesses.

Lunar Abundance Spell is a testament to the power of manifestation and the power of the mind to attract positive energies into one's life. By focusing your thoughts and energy on abundance and prosperity, you create a vibration that attracts those energies into your life. By performing the spell during a full moon, you tap into the powerful energies of the moon for added potency.

You will need the following:

- green candle
- one piece of paper and pen
- a bowl of water
- a citrine crystal or jade

To perform the spell, follow these steps:

1. Preparation: Choose a night when there is a full moon, and set up a workspace in a quiet room.
2. Cleanse Your Space: Light some incense or smudge the room with sage to cleanse the space and remove any negative energies. This helps to create a positive and supportive environment for your spell.
3. Light the Candle: Light the green candle and place it on a table in front of you. The green candle symbolizes growth, abundance, and prosperity.
4. Write Your Intentions: On the piece of paper, write your intention for wealth and prosperity. Be specific about what you desire, and focus on the feeling of abundance and financial stability.
5. Place the Paper in the Bowl of Water: Place the piece of paper in the bowl of water, letting it soak for a few moments. The water symbolizes the flow of abundance into your life.
6. Visualize Your Intentions: Hold the crystals or stones in your hands and close your eyes. Visualize yourself surrounded by wealth and prosperity, and feel the energy of abundance and financial stability flowing into your life. Repeat the following incantation:

   "By the power of the lunar light, Bring abundance into my sight. With this spell, I call upon, Wealth and prosperity now. So mote it be."

7. Seal the Spell: When you feel that you have connected with the energies of abundance and prosperity, blow out the candle and place the piece of paper in a safe place, such as a money jar or a special box. The spell is sealed, and the energies of abundance will continue to work for you.

MONEY DRAWING SPELL

The Money Drawing Spell is a Wiccan spell used to attract wealth, prosperity, and abundance into one's life. It is often performed during the full moon or when the moon is in the sign of Taurus or Leo, which are associated with money and wealth.

In Wicca, the Money Drawing Spell is often seen as a form of manifestation magic, where the practitioner uses their will and intention to bring their desires into reality. It is believed that the power of the spell lies in the practitioner's ability to focus their intention and visualize their desired outcome rather than in any specific words or materials used.

Some Wiccans believe the spell should be performed with caution, as it may have unintended consequences if not done with integrity and a clear intention. It is essential to approach the spell with gratitude and understand that abundance and prosperity come from various sources, not just material wealth.

You will need the following:
- A green candle
- A piece of green cloth or paper
- A pen
- Anointing oil (such as olive oil or sandalwood oil)
- Cinnamon or bay leaves (fresh or dried)
- A fire-safe dish or holder for the candle
- A small coin or piece of gold

To perform the spell, follow these steps:

1. Set up your altar or a quiet, private space where you will perform the spell. Place the green candle in the holder, and lay the green cloth or paper next to it.
2. Anoint the candle with the anointing oil, starting at the wick and working your way down to the base of the candle. As you anoint the candle, visualize your intention for financial abundance and prosperity.
3. Light the candle, and scatter the cinnamon or bay leaves around the base of the candle.
4. Using the pen, write down your intention on the green cloth or paper. This could be a specific financial goal or desire or a general statement such as "I release all negative thoughts and beliefs about money, and I choose to focus on abundance and prosperity. I am confident and capable of attracting wealth and abundance into my life."
5. Hold your hands over the candle and the piece of paper, and speak your intention out loud. Visualize the green light of the candle enveloping you, filling you with positivity and financial abundance. Repeat your intention several times until you feel a strong connection with the energy of the spell.
6. Place the small coin or piece of gold on top of the piece of paper with your intention and speak the words:
   "Money, come to me. Bring abundance and prosperity. With open heart and clear intention, I call forth wealth and financial success. I am worthy and deserving, And I trust in the universe to provide. By the power of this spell, I manifest abundance and prosperity, Now and always. So mote it be."
7. Allow the candle to burn down completely, and keep the piece of paper with your intention and coin somewhere safe.

GREEN LIGHT SPELL

The Green Light Spell is a spell commonly used in Wiccan magic for success, growth, and manifestation. This spell is often used to harness the power of nature and the elements to bring abundance, prosperity, and good fortune into one's life.

The use of green as a symbol of abundance and prosperity can be found in many cultures throughout history. In ancient Egypt, for example, green was associated with the goddess Isis, who was revered as a symbol of fertility, abundance, and prosperity. The Celts also saw green as a symbol of growth and abundance, and used it in their celebrations of the spring equinox.

Green is also associated with the element of earth, which represents stability, grounding, and practicality. By combining the energy of the green candle with your written intention and spoken words, you are creating a powerful manifestation tool that can help bring your desired outcomes into reality.

You will need the following:

- A green candle (representing growth and abundance)
- A piece of green cloth or paper (to wrap around the candle)
- A green stone such as peridot or aventurine (to represent growth and abundance)
- A lighter or matches

To perform the spell, follow these steps:

1. Begin by setting up your altar or working space. You may want to include items that symbolize growth, abundance, and prosperity to you, such as plants, herbs, or symbols of wealth.
2. Wrap the green cloth or paper around the green candle, securing it in place. Place the green stone on top of the cloth-wrapped candle.
3. Light the candle and focus your energy and intention on the flame. Visualize the green light of the candle filling your space, bringing growth, abundance, and prosperity into your life.
4. Hold the green stone in your hands and repeat the following incantation:

   "Green light of growth, Bring abundance to me. Fertile soil and thriving crops, Prosperity and good fortune, So mote it be."

5. Focus your energy and intention on the green stone and visualize the energy of the spell spreading out into the world, manifesting your desires and bringing abundance into your life.
6. Allow the candle to burn down completely, using the green light to symbolize the growth and abundance that you are calling into your life.
7. Keep the green stone with you when the candle has burned down as a talisman of the spell's energy.

MOON PHASE ABUNDANCE SPELL

This spell has a rich history that dates back to the ancient times of the Celts. The Celts believed that the moon held a great power that could be harnessed to bring abundance into one's life. They would perform this spell during the waxing moon phase, when the moon was growing, just like they wanted their abundance to grow.

One legendary story of the Moon Phase Abundance Spell tells of a young woman named Aine, who lived in poverty and longed for a better life. She came across a wise old woman who taught her the spell and advised her to perform it during the waxing moon phase. Aine followed the instructions and was amazed at the results. She soon found herself surrounded by abundance in all forms and lived a happy and prosperous life.

Years passed, and Aine became known as the "Wealthy One" and was sought out by many who sought to learn her secret. Aine was happy to share the spell and the story of how she came to learn it, but she warned them that the spell could only bring abundance if they truly believed in it and the power of the moon.

You will need the following:

- 1 groon oandlo
- 1 piece of rose quartz

- 1 piece of citrine
- 1 sprig of rosemary
- 1 tablespoon of basil
- 1 tablespoon of cinnamon
- 1 tablespoon of nutmeg
- 1 tablespoon of sugar
- 1 tablespoon of honey
- A lighter or matches

To perform the spell, follow these steps:

1. Gather all of your ingredients in one place.
2. Cleanse and bless your ingredients, as well as yourself, by holding each item in your hands and visualizing the white light surrounding them.
3. On a flat surface, place your green candle in the center and arrange the rose quartz and citrine on either side of it.
4. Sprinkle the sprig of rosemary, basil, cinnamon, nutmeg, sugar, and honey around the candle.
5. Light the green candle and close your eyes. Take several deep breaths, focusing on your intention to bring abundance into your life.
6. Repeat the following incantation three times:

   "By the power of the moon, I call upon the universe to bring abundance into my life. So mote it be."

7. Hold your hands over the candle, rose quartz, and citrine, and visualize yourself surrounded by abundance in all forms.
8. Allow the candle to burn down completely, but make sure to supervise it and keep it away from any flammable materials.
9. Keep the rose quartz and citrine in your home to continue attracting abundance.

ABUNDANCE BATH SPELL

The Abundance Bath Spell is a ritual performed in Wicca to promote prosperity, abundance, and financial stability. The spell involves creating a bath infused with symbols, herbs, and oils believed to attract abundance and good luck.

In Wicca, it is believed that the power of manifestation is enhanced through ritual and intention. By performing the Abundance Bath Spell, you are setting the intention to attract abundance and financial stability into your life.

Additionally, it is essential to note that attracting abundance is not just about money but about having an abundance of all good things in life, including love, health, and happiness. By focusing your energy on abundance and prosperity, you are sending out a positive message to the universe and opening yourself up to receive all the good things that life has to offer.

It is also important to practice gratitude and generosity as part of your abundance practice. Acknowledge the good things in your life, no matter how small, and show appreciation for them. Give back to others and share your abundance with others, as this will help attract even more abundance into your life.

The Abundance Bath Spell can be performed as often as you like. Still, it is recommended to perform it once a week or during important financial times, such as when you are seeking a new job or making an important financial decision.

Remember that the power of spells like this comes from within, and it is crucial to have a positive and open mindset while performing the spell. Trust in the universe and the power of manifestation to bring abundance into your life. With time, patience, and persistence, you will see positive results.

You will need the following:

- Rose petals, basil, mint, lavender, and jasmine flowers
- A green candle
- A coin or piece of green paper
- Bottle of olive oil or cinnamon oil

To perform the spell, follow these steps:

1. Cleanse your space: Before you begin, it is important to cleanse your space of any negative energy. You can do this by burning sage or palo santo or by simply opening windows and doors to let fresh air in.
2. Draw a bath: Fill your bathtub with warm water, making sure that the water level is high enough to cover your body.
3. Add the herbs: Take the rose petals, basil, mint, lavender, and jasmine flowers and sprinkle them into the bathtub. These herbs are believed to attract abundance and good luck.

4. Light the green candle: Light the green candle and place it on a safe and stable surface near the bathtub. Green is the color associated with abundance and financial stability in Wicca.

5. Add the oil: Take the bottle of olive oil or cinnamon oil and pour a generous amount into the bath. These oils are believed to bring wealth and prosperity.

6. Place the coin or green paper in the bath: Take the coin or green piece of paper and place it in the bathtub, symbolizing abundance and wealth.

7. Get into the bath: Slowly get into the bathtub, making sure that you are surrounded by herbs, oils, and symbols. Soak in the bath for at least 15-20 minutes, allowing the herbs, oils, and symbols to envelop you.

8. Visualize abundance: While in the bath, close your eyes and focus on your intention for abundance and financial stability. Visualize yourself surrounded by prosperity and abundance. See yourself having all the financial stability and abundance you need and desire. Repeat the mantra:

"I am abundant, I am financially stable, and prosperity flows to me."

9. Dispose of the materials: When you are finished with the bath, dispose of the herbs, candle, and any other materials in a safe and respectful manner. Do not reuse the bath water.

10. Light a new green candle: Light a new green candle and let it burn down completely. Repeat the affirmations or mantras you used while in the bath, focusing on your intention for abundance and financial stability.

11. Close the spell: When the candle has burned down, blow it out and say,

"So mote it be." This is a traditional Wiccan phrase used to close a spell and seal its energy.

MONEY CHARM SPELL

The Wicca Money Charm Spell is a spell used in Wiccan magic to attract financial abundance and prosperity into one's life. This spell is often performed using a charm or talisman, which is a physical object imbued with magical energy and intent. Charms and talismans can be carried with you or placed in a prominent location as a reminder of your financial goals and as a symbol of your manifestation efforts.

The history of the Wicca Money Charm Spell is challenging to trace, as the origins of Wiccan magic and spell-casting are shrouded in mystery and folklore. Wicca is a modern religion that draws upon ancient pagan beliefs, and the use of charms and talismans for manifestation and protection is a common practice in many cultures throughout history.

The use of charms and talismans for financial prosperity specifically can be found in various ancient civilizations, such as the Egyptians, who believed that carrying certain symbols or stones would bring financial abundance. In medieval Europe, it was common for merchants and traders to carry small amulets or talismans to attract wealth and success in their business endeavors.

The Wicca Money Charm Spell, as it is known today, is likely a modern adaptation of these ancient traditions combined with the principles and practices of Wicca. In Wicca, the

use of charms and talismans is seen as a way to focus and amplify one's intention and energy and physically represent one's desires.

You will need the following:

- Green candle
- Bay leaves
- Cinnamon sticks
- Money oil or peppermint oil
- A green cloth or piece of paper

To perform the spell, follow these steps:

1. Cleanse your space and yourself with sage or palo santo to remove any negative energy.
2. Light the green candle and place it in front of you.
3. Place the bay leaves and cinnamon sticks in a small bowl or on a plate and sprinkle with a few drops of oil.
4. Wrap the bay leaves and cinnamon sticks in the green cloth or paper and tie them with a string.
5. Hold the cloth or paper in your hands and close your eyes. Visualize yourself surrounded by abundance and financial prosperity.
6. Repeat the following chant three times:

   "Money come to me, fast and free. Prosperity and wealth, blessed be. By the power of the earth and sea, So mote it be!"

7. Place the cloth or paper near the candle and let it burn down completely.
8. Keep the cloth or paper in a safe place where you will see it often to reinforce the spell.

FINANCIAL FREEDOM SPELL

The Financial Freedom Spell is a spell specific to Wiccan magic that is used to break free from financial difficulties, increase abundance, and promote financial stability. This spell is often performed during the Waxing Moon phase when the energy of the moon is growing and increasing, symbolizing growth and prosperity in one's financial situation.

The Waxing Moon phase is the period of time between the New Moon and the Full Moon when the moon is increasing in size and visibility. During this phase, the moon moves from being a thin crescent to being fully illuminated.

Many Wiccans see the Financial Freedom Spell as an opportunity to align their personal values with their financial goals. This involves creating a clear vision of what financial stability and independence means to them and using the spell to help manifest that vision into reality.

The spell can also be used as a form of self-reflection and personal growth. By focusing on abundance and prosperity, the practitioner can identify and release any limiting beliefs or patterns of behavior that may be blocking their financial success.

You will need the following:

- A green candle
- A piece of paper or parchment paper
- A pen
- Anointing oil (such as olive oil or cinnamon oil)
- Patchouli or frankincense essential oil
- Cloves, cinnamon sticks, or bay leaves
- A fire-safe dish or holder for the candle

To perform the spell, follow these steps:

1. Set up your altar or a quiet, private space where you will perform the spell. Place the green candle in the holder, and lay the piece of paper next to it.
2. Anoint the candle with the anointing oil, starting at the wick and working your way down to the base of the candle. As you anoint the candle, visualize yourself breaking free from financial difficulties and increasing your abundance.
3. Light the candle, and sprinkle the cloves, cinnamon sticks, or bay leaves around the base of the candle.
4. Write down your intention for financial freedom on the piece of paper, using the pen. This could be a specific amount of debt you want to pay off, a statement of your financial goals, or a general intention for financial stability and abundance.
5. Hold your hands over the candle and the piece of paper, and speak your intention out loud. Visualize the green light of the candle filling you with positive energy and breaking any negative financial cycles or patterns. Repeat your intention several times until you feel a strong connection with the energy of the spell.
6. Drop a few drops of patchouli or frankincense essential oil onto the candle and onto the piece of paper and repeat the following incantation:

"Goddess of abundance, hear my plea. Bring financial stability and freedom to me. With the power of the waxing moon, I call upon your energies. Soon, I release all fear and lack And invite prosperity to come back. I am open to receiving your gifts And commit to using them for the greater good, with no shift, So mote it be."

This will help to purify and bless the spell and to enhance its manifestation.

7. Allow the candle to burn down completely, and keep the piece of paper with your intention somewhere safe. You can also bury the paper in the ground or burn it in a safe, fire-proof container, releasing the energy of the spell into the universe.

PINECONE SPELL

The history of the Pinecone Spell is rooted in the ancient belief that pinecones held the power of abundance and prosperity. Pinecones were often used as symbols of the harvest and fertility and were associated with the goddesses of abundance and wealth in many cultures. The use of pinecones in magic can be traced back to the ancient Egyptians, who incorporated pinecones into their religious practices as symbols of resurrection and life.

The Pinecone Spell combines the energy of the pinecone with the power of intention and visualization to help bring abundance and prosperity into the practitioner's life. By writing down a specific financial goal or intention, wrapping the pinecone with a green ribbon, and focusing on the goal as the ribbon is tied, the practitioner is able to tap into the powerful energy of the universe and attract wealth and prosperity.

In the tradition of Wicca, the Pinecone Spell is often performed during the fall or winter, when the energy of the earth is focused on rest and renewal. The spell is also commonly performed during the celebration of Samhain, a festival that marks the end of the harvest and symbolizes the beginning of a new cycle of growth and abundance.

You will need the following:

- A large pinecone
- Green ribbon or string
- A piece of paper and pen
- Optional: Essential oils such as frankincense or sandalwood to anoint the pinecone

To perform the spell, follow these steps:

1. Cleanse and prepare the space. Begin by cleaning and purifying the space where you will perform the spell. You can do this by smudging with sage or palo santo or by using a saltwater bath. This will help to clear any negative energy and create a positive and receptive atmosphere for your spellwork.
2. Anoint the pinecone Optional: Anoint the pinecone with essential oils that correspond to abundance, such as frankincense or sandalwood. This will help to infuse the pinecone with positive energy and enhance the spell's effectiveness.
3. Write your intention. Take a piece of paper and write down your intention for this spell. This could be a specific financial goal, such as increasing your income or paying off debt, or a more general desire for financial stability and abundance.
4. Wrap the pinecone with a green ribbon. Wrap the green ribbon around the pinecone, tying it tightly. As you do this, speak the words:

"By the power of earth and nature's might, I call upon the spirits of light. With this pinecone, sacred and true, I cast this spell just for me and you.
Oh, ancient powers of growth and change, Bring forth your magic, rearrange. This pinecone symbolizes my intent, To manifest my desires to the full extent.

So let it be, let it be done, so mote it be with harm to none and love for everyone. This spell is cast, this spell is bound. With magic's power, it shall be found."

5. Place the pinecone in a prominent location, such as on your altar or in a place where you will see it often. This will help to keep your intention and visualization at the forefront of your mind.
6. Repeat the spell as desired. Repeat the spell as often as you like, either daily or weekly, depending on your goals and needs. Over time, as you continue to focus on your intention and visualization, you may begin to see positive changes in your financial situation.

MYSTICAL MEDICINES

HEALING OF ADDICTION AND COMPULSIVE BEHAVIORS

The Healing of Addiction and Compulsive Behaviors spell is a powerful Wiccan spell used to overcome the negative effects of addictive and compulsive behaviors.

The Healing of Addiction and Compulsive Behaviors spell is said to have originated from a group of ancient Wiccan healers who lived deep in the forests of the Celtic region. The healers observed the struggles of those around them who were grappling with addiction and compulsive behaviors and felt deep compassion for their suffering. They were determined to find a way to help, and so they began experimenting with different herbs, crystals, and incantations to create a spell that could break the hold of addiction and compulsive behavior.

After many years of trial and error, the healers finally discovered the perfect combination of ingredients and incantations that would banish addiction and compulsive behavior for good. They called their spell the "Healing of Addiction and Compulsive Behaviors," and it quickly became renowned throughout the Wiccan community for its effectiveness. The spell was passed down from generation to generation and is now widely used by Wiccan healers all over the world.

You will need the following:

- Seven rose petals
- One green candle
- Three drops of lavender essential oil
- One piece of rose quartz
- One piece of amethyst
- Salt
- Incense (Frankincense, Myrrh, Sandalwood)

To perform the spell, follow these steps:

1. Cleanse the area you will be performing the spell in. You can do this by burning the incense or spreading salt around the room.
2. Light the green candle.
3. Place the rose petals in front of the candle.
4. Place the rose quartz and amethyst on top of the rose petals.
5. Place the lavender essential oil on your palms and inhale its aroma.
6. Repeat the following incantation 3 times:

    "With the essence of earth, air, fire, and water, I call upon the divine forces of the universe. I implore the energy of the moon, the wisdom of the stars, and the power of the sun to guide me at this moment. I banish the hold that addiction and compulsive behaviors have over me and ask that they be replaced with strength, clarity, and balance. Let the power of my intention be strengthened and amplified by the forces of nature. I invite positive change and growth to fill my being, and I vow to embrace this transformation with grace and courage. So mote it be."

7. Hold the rose quartz and amethyst in your hands, and visualize yourself being free from addiction and compulsive behaviors.

8. When you feel the energy of the spell is complete, blow out the candle and allow the rose petals to wilt away naturally.
9. Note: This spell should be performed during a time when the moon is in its waxing phase, as this symbolizes growth and renewal.

HEALING OF GRIEF AND LOSS SPELL

The Healing of Grief and Loss spell is a powerful Wiccan ritual that is used to help individuals move through their grief and find peace and comfort. The spell is designed to help release negative emotions and promote healing and growth. This spell can be performed on one's own or with a coven. It is a powerful spell that is used to help those who are struggling with feelings of grief and loss to heal and move forward in their lives. The spell is believed to have originated in ancient times when people would gather in groups to perform rituals and spells to help them cope with the various challenges they faced in their lives.

One of the earliest known practitioners of this spell was a wise woman who lived in the countryside. She was known for her ability to help people who were struggling with grief and loss, and she would often perform this spell for those who came to her seeking help. The spell was passed down from generation to generation, and it became a staple of Wiccan practice for those who sought to heal their hearts and minds.

You will need the following:

- White candle
- Herbs for grief, such as lavender, rose petals, or chamomile
- A piece of rose quartz
- An incense burner or smudge stick
- Matches or a lighter
- A piece of paper and a pen

To perform the spell, follow these steps:

1. Cleanse the space: Before performing the spell, it is important to cleanse the area of negative energy. This can be done by smudging the space with sage or palo santo or by using incense such as frankincense or myrrh.
2. Cast a circle: Cast a protective circle by visualizing white light surrounding you. This will keep negative energy out and provide a safe space for the spell.
3. Light the candle: Light the white candle and place it in front of you. This candle represents the light of healing and the release of negativity.
4. Place the herbs: Sprinkle the herbs around the candle, representing the release of grief and sorrow.
5. Hold the rose quartz: Hold the piece of rose quartz in your hands and close your eyes. Visualize the energy of the stone, filling you with comfort and peace.
6. Write down your grief: Take the piece of paper and pen and write down what you are grieving. This can be a person, a situation, or an emotion. Allow yourself to fully feel your grief as you write.
7. Burn the paper: Once you have written down your grief, fold the paper and place it in the incense burner or smudge stick. Light it, and allow the paper to burn completely, releasing your grief and negativity and speaking the words:

"Oh, elements of air, fire, water, earth, and spirit, hear my plea. I am grieving and in pain, but I seek comfort and peace. With this candle, I release my sorrow and negativity. With these herbs, I heal my heart and find solace. With this rose quartz, I am filled with comfort and love. As I burn this paper, I let go of my grief and invite positive change. So mote it be."

8. Close the circle: Thank the elements and the universe for their help and guidance. Close the circle by visualizing the white light fading away.
9. Extinguish the candle: Extinguish the candle and dispose of the ashes and herbs. Hold the rose quartz close, allowing its energy to continue to comfort and heal you.

HEALING OF INSOMNIA AND SLEEP DISORDERS SPELL

The Healing of Insomnia and Sleep Disorders spell is a spell that has been used for centuries in Wicca magic to help those who suffer from insomnia and sleep disorders find rest and peace. This spell is designed to calm the mind, soothe the spirit, and bring about peaceful restful sleep. The spell dates back to ancient times when a wise village woman used her knowledge of herbs and magic to help those in need.

One such story tells of a young woman named Aella, who had been plagued by insomnia and sleep disorders for as long as she could remember. Despite seeking the help of various healers and doctors, nothing seemed to bring her the peace and rest she so desperately sought.

One day, Aella stumbled upon a gathering of Wiccan healers and was immediately drawn to their wisdom and knowledge. She approached them, sharing her story and begging for their help. The healers listened with compassion, and after much discussion, they came up with a spell designed specifically to help Aella overcome her insomnia and sleep disorders.

The spell was simple yet powerful, involving the use of herbs such as lavender and chamomile, as well as the recitation of an incantation that called upon the power of the moon and the restful energy of the earth. As Aella performed the spell, she could feel the tension and stress leaving her body, replaced by a sense of calm and serenity.

Over the course of several nights, Aella performed the spell, and to her amazement, she began to sleep soundly and peacefully. The restful sleep she received each night brought her a renewed sense of energy and vitality, and she was soon able to return to her normal life, free from the grip of insomnia and sleep disorders.

From that day forward, the Healing of Insomnia and Sleep Disorders spell became a staple in the Wiccan community, passed down from generation to generation, and used to help those in need find peace and rest. The spell remains a powerful tool for those seeking to overcome insomnia and sleep disorders and reclaim their health and vitality.

You will need the following:

- A white candle
- A piece of amethyst or rose quartz
- Lavender or chamomile essential oil
- A pen and paper
- A lighter or matches

To perform the spell, follow these steps:

1. Find a quiet, peaceful place where you will not be disturbed. Light the white candle and place it on a flat surface in front of you.
2. Take a moment to ground and center yourself. Close your eyes and take deep breaths, focusing on the present moment.
3. Place the piece of amethyst or rose quartz on top of the candle. This crystal is said to have a calming energy that can help with sleep issues.
4. Anoint the candle with the lavender or chamomile essential oil, focusing on the intention of bringing peace and restful sleep.
5. Write down your fears, worries, or any thoughts that may be keeping you awake on the piece of paper.
6. Hold the paper in your hands, close your eyes, and repeat the incantation:

   "By the light of the moon, I release the worries of the day. With the energy of the stars, I banish insomnia and invite restful slumber. The universe guides me, the universe protects me, and the universe brings me peace. I call upon the powers of nature, the wind, the earth, the fire, and the water, to aid in my quest for restful sleep. Let my dreams be filled with peace and serenity. Let my mind be free from the chaos of the world. So mote it be, so shall it be done."

7. Roll the paper and tie it with a ribbon or string. Place it under the candle.
8. Watch the candle burn down completely, visualizing a peaceful and restful sleep. When the candle has burned down, dispose of the paper in a way that feels appropriate to you.
9. Go to bed feeling calm and rested, knowing that you have invited peace and restful sleep into your life.

HEALING OF PAST TRAUMAS OR HURTFUL EXPERIENCES SPELL

The Healing of Past Traumas or Hurtful Experiences spell is a powerful ritual used by Wiccan practitioners to help release negative emotions and energy associated with past experiences that still cause pain or distress. It is said that the spell originated from a powerful Wiccan healer named Althea, who lived deep in the forest.

Althea was renowned for her exceptional ability to heal individuals from the physical and emotional scars of their past. However, one day, she encountered a young woman who was suffering from a deep-rooted trauma that no amount of physical healing could cure. Althea knew that she needed to delve into the spiritual realm to heal the woman's mind, body, and soul.

After much contemplation and meditation, Althea discovered that the root cause of the woman's pain was tied to her past traumas and hurtful experiences. With this knowledge, Althea created the Healing of past traumas or hurtful experiences spell, which aimed to provide a spiritual release from the pain of past experiences and allow individuals to heal and move forward in their lives.

The spell calls upon the power of the elements, including air, fire, water, earth, and spirit, to bring balance and harmony to mind, body, and soul. The spell also calls upon the energy of the moon and stars to heal the individual's spirit and provide the strength needed to move forward.

You will need the following:

- White candles (2)
- Rose petals (dried or fresh)
- Frankincense resin
- Sage or lavender incense
- Matches or a lighter
- A quiet and private space to perform the spell
- A piece of paper and pen

To perform the spell, follow these steps:

1. Set the stage: Clear your space, light the sage or lavender incense, and place the candles in front of you.
2. Write down the trauma or hurtful experience: Take the piece of paper and pen and write down the specific event or experience that still haunts you. Be as detailed as possible, but do not judge yourself or dwell on negative emotions. Simply acknowledge the experience.
3. Light the candles: Light the white candles using the matches or lighter, and focus your energy on the flame.
4. Burn the piece of paper: Take the piece of paper with the written experience and burn it over the flame of the candles. As you watch the paper burn, visualize the negative emotions and memories associated with the experience being released.

5. Sprinkle rose petals: Sprinkle the rose petals over the burning paper and ashes, symbolizing love and compassion towards yourself.
6. Burn the frankincense: Burn the frankincense resin and focus on the smoke, which will help to purify the energy and space.
7. Recite the incantation: Chant the following incantation with intention and focus:

   "By the grace of the earth beneath my feet, and the wisdom of the ancient trees, I banish these traumas of the past. By the light of the moon, and the gentleness of the winds, I cleanse my mind and heart of their hold. By the power of the universe, and the love it holds, I call upon its energy to heal these wounds and bring peace. So mote it be."

8. Extinguish the candles: Once the incantation is complete, extinguish the candles and allow the incense to burn out.

HEALING OF FERTILITY ISSUES SPELL

The Healing of Reproductive Health and Fertility Issues spell is a powerful and intricate spell that is used to address and overcome issues related to reproductive health and fertility. In ancient times, women would come together in secret to perform spells and rituals to honor the goddesses of fertility and ask for their blessings in conceiving a child. Over time, these rituals evolved into the Healing of Reproductive Health and Fertility Issues spell, a powerful spell that has been passed down through generations of Wiccan practitioners.

The spell is said to have originated from a wise woman named Lava, who lived in a small village surrounded by rolling hills and fertile fields. Lava was known for her ability to connect with the natural world and was often sought after by couples struggling with fertility issues. She would perform a ritual in which she would call upon the goddesses of fertility and ask for their blessings. Lava would then anoint the couple with oils and herbs that were believed to increase fertility and invite positive energy into their lives.

You will need the following:

- A pink candle
- A green candle
- Essential oil blend of clary sage, lavender, and rose
- Dried rose petals
- Dried chamomile flowers
- A piece of rose quartz
- A piece of green aventurine
- A chalice filled with spring water

To perform the spell, follow these steps:

1. Cast a circle of protection around your space and call upon the elements of Earth, Air, Fire, Water, and Spirit.
2. Light the pink candle and say, "With the power of the goddess of fertility, I call upon you to bless this ritual."
3. Anoint the pink candle with the essential oil blend and place it in the center of your altar.
4. Sprinkle the dried rose petals around the pink candle.
5. Light the green candle and say, "With the power of the god of growth and life, I call upon you to bless this ritual."
6. Anoint the green candle with the essential oil blend and place it beside the pink candle.
7. Sprinkle the dried chamomile flowers around the green candle.
8. Hold the rose quartz in your hands and say, "With the love and light of the universe, I invite healing and balance into my reproductive health."
9. Place the rose quartz in front of the pink candle.
10. Hold the green aventurine in your hands and say, "With the strength and power of nature, I invite growth and fertility into my life."
11. Place the green aventurine in front of the green candle.

12. Pick up the chalice of spring water and say:

"By the power of the moon, I call upon the ancient wisdom To heal and balance my reproductive system. With the gentle touch of rose petals, I invite peace and calm. With the fragrant scent of lavender, I call forth healing energy. With the energy of rose quartz, I invite love and light. With the grounding force of sandalwood, I bring balance and stability. By the power of the earth, I release any blockages or obstacles With the strength of the sky. I banish any negative energy. With the love of the universe, I invite fertility and health into me."

13. Take a sip from the chalice and sprinkle the rest of the water around your altar.
14. Close your eyes and visualize yourself surrounded by a warm, comforting light. See yourself as healthy and whole, with a body that is able to conceive and carry a child.
15. When you feel ready, blow out the pink and green candles and say, "So mote it be."
16. Close the circle of protection and give thanks to the elements.

CHAKRA HARMONIES

THROAT CHAKRA BALANCING SPELL

The Throat Chakra Balancing Spell is a powerful ritual used to align and balance the fifth chakra, also known as the Throat Chakra. This chakra governs communication, self-expression, and creativity and is associated with the color blue. When the Throat Chakra is balanced, individuals are able to express themselves authentically and effectively, and they have a greater ability to communicate their thoughts, feelings, and desires.

According to legend, the Throat Chakra Balancing Spell was first practiced by a wise and mystical priestess who lived in the lush and verdant forests of the East. This priestess was known for her ability to communicate with the spirits of the earth and sky, and her wisdom was sought after by all who knew her.

One day, as the priestess was meditating in a quiet glade, she heard a soft voice calling to her from the forest. She followed the voice and soon came upon a small clearing where she saw a vision of a brilliant blue light shining from the throat of a woman. The priestess was struck by the power and beauty of this light, and she knew in her heart that it was a symbol of the Throat Chakra.

With this newfound understanding, the priestess set out to create a spell to align and balance the Throat Chakra. She gathered blue candles, blue crystals, and essential oils and performed the ritual under the light of the full moon. As she repeated the incantation, she felt powerful energy flowing through her, and she knew that the spell was working.

From that day forward, the priestess taught the Throat Chakra Balancing Spell to her followers, and it soon spread throughout the land, becoming a popular practice among those seeking to improve their communication, self-expression, and creativity.

You will need the following:

- Blue candles
- Blue crystals, such as turquoise or aquamarine
- Essential oils, such as eucalyptus or peppermint
- Matches or a lighter
- A serene and quiet space
- A comfortable place to sit or lie down

To perform the spell, follow these steps:

1. Cleanse and prepare your space by lighting incense or using a smudge stick. This will help to purify the energy and create a peaceful environment for your spell.
2. Set up your workspace by placing the blue candles on either side of you and the blue crystals in front of you.
3. Anoint the candles and crystals with a few drops of essential oil, focusing on your intention to balance the Throat Chakra.

4. Light the candles, and take a few deep breaths to calm and center yourself.
5. Close your eyes and visualize a bright blue light shining from your throat area.
6. Repeat the following incantation:

"By the power of the universe, I call upon the energies of the Throat Chakra. I ask that you align and balance my ability to communicate and express myself. Let the blue light of the candles and the peace of the crystals guide me on my path. So mote it be."

7. Hold the crystals and visualize them absorbing any negative or blocked energy from your Throat Chakra. Replace any negative energy with the light and love of the universe.
8. Continue to visualize the blue light shining from your Throat Chakra, and feel it expanding and growing in strength.
9. When you feel ready, extinguish the candles and carefully store the crystals.

CHAKRA BALANCING SPELL FOR ALL 7 CHAKRAS

The Chakra Balancing Spell for All 7 Chakras is a powerful and transformative ritual that has been practiced for centuries within the Wiccan tradition. This spell is designed to balance and align all seven of the body's chakras, which are spinning energy centers that regulate the flow of energy throughout the body. When all of the chakras are balanced and aligned, the practitioner is said to experience greater physical, emotional, and spiritual well-being.

The Chakra Balancing Spell for All 7 Chakras has its roots in ancient Wiccan traditions. It is said that long ago, a wise and powerful Wiccan priestess discovered the secret of the chakras, seven spinning wheels of energy located along the spine, each governing different aspects of a person's physical, emotional, and spiritual well-being.

However, she soon realized that many people struggled to maintain balance in all of their chakras and as a result, were unable to fully realize their potential. With a deep understanding of the power of magic, the priestess created a spell to balance all seven chakras so that individuals could tap into their full potential and live fulfilling abundant lives.

You will need the following:

- Seven candles in the colors associated with each of the seven chakras: red, orange, yellow, green, blue, indigo, and violet
- Seven crystals or gemstones associated with each of the seven chakras: garnet, carnelian, citrine, peridot, aquamarine, lapis lazuli, and amethyst
- Essential oils associated with each of the seven chakras: sandalwood, peppermint, lemon, eucalyptus, lavender, frankincense, and lotus
- Mat or cushion for sitting
- Quiet, private space

To perform the spell, follow these steps:

1. Set up your space by lighting the seven candles and placing the seven crystals or gemstones in front of them.
2. Sit comfortably on your mat or cushion, close your eyes, and take several deep breaths to calm your mind and body.
3. Begin with the root chakra, which is associated with the color red and is located at the base of the spine. Anoint the root chakra candle with sandalwood essential oil, and hold the garnet crystal in your hand. Repeat the following incantation:

   "By the power of the universe, I call upon the energies of the root chakra. I ask that you balance and align my foundation, stability, and security. Let the warmth of the garnet and the earthy aroma of sandalwood guide me on my path. So mote it be."

4. Move on to the sacral chakra, which is associated with the color orange and is located in the lower abdomen. Anoint the sacral chakra candle with peppermint essential oil, and hold the carnelian crystal in your hand. Repeat the following incantation:

"By the power of the universe, I call upon the energies of the sacral chakra. I ask that you balance and align my passions, desires, and sensuality. Let the energy of the carnelian and the refreshing scent of peppermint guide me on my path. So mote it be."

5. Continue with the solar plexus chakra, which is associated with the color yellow and is located in the upper abdomen. Anoint the solar plexus chakra candle with lemon essential oil, and hold the citrine crystal in your hand. Repeat the following incantation:

   "By the power of the universe, I call upon the energies of the solar plexus chakra. I ask that you balance and align my confidence, self-esteem, and power. Let the light of the citrine and the zesty aroma of lemon guide me on my path. So mote it be."

6. Move on to the heart chakra, which is associated with the color green and is located in the center of the chest. Anoint the heart chakra candle with eucalyptus essential oil, and hold the peridot crystal in your hand. Repeat the following incantation:

   "By the power of the universe, I call upon the energies of the heart chakra. I ask that you balance and align my love, compassion, and connection. Let the energy of the peridot and the invigorating aroma of eucalyptus guide me on my path. So mote it be."

7. Continue with the throat chakra, which is associated with the color blue and is located in the throat. Anoint the throat chakra candle with lavender essential oil, and hold the aquamarine crystal in your hand. Repeat the following incantation:

"By the power of the universe, I call upon the energies of the throat chakra. I ask that you balance and align my ability to communicate and express myself. Let the tranquility of the aquamarine and the soothing scent of lavender guide me on my path. So mote it be."

8. Move on to the third eye chakra, which is associated with the color indigo and is located between the eyebrows. Anoint the third eye chakra candle with frankincense essential oil, and hold the lapis lazuli crystal in your hand. Repeat the following incantation:

"By the power of the universe, I call upon the energies of the third eye chakra. I ask that you balance and align my intuition, psychic abilities, and wisdom. Let the wisdom of the lapis lazuli and the mystical aroma of frankincense guide me on my path. So mote it be."

9. Finish with the crown chakra, which is associated with the color violet and is located at the top of the head. Anoint the crown chakra candle with lotus essential oil, and hold the amethyst crystal in your hand. Repeat the following incantation:

"By the power of the universe, I call upon the energies of the crown chakra. I ask that you balance and align my spirituality, enlightenment, and connection to the divine. Let the peace of the amethyst and the calming aroma of lotus guide me on my path. So mote it be."

10. After completing the incantations for each chakra, sit quietly for a few moments and allow the energies to settle. When you feel ready, slowly open your eyes and blow out each of the candles.

SOLAR PLEXUS CHAKRA BALANCING SPELL

The Solar Plexus Chakra Balancing Spell is a powerful tool for Wiccans looking to bring balance to their third chakra, located in the area of the solar plexus. This chakra governs self-esteem, personal power, and the ability to take action in the world, making it a key player in our overall well-being.

The Solar Plexus Chakra Balancing Spell has its roots in ancient Wiccan tradition and is believed to have been first performed by wise women and healers in the pagan communities of Europe. According to legend, these women noticed that some individuals in their communities seemed to be constantly struggling with feelings of low self-esteem, fear, and insecurity. They realized that these individuals had a blocked Solar Plexus Chakra, the center of personal power and self-esteem, located in the stomach area.

In response to this, wise women and healers developed the Solar Plexus Chakra Balancing Spell, which involved calling upon the energies of the Solar Plexus Chakra and asking for its alignment and balance. They used various tools, such as the bright yellow of the citrine crystal and the energizing scent of the ginger essential oil, to aid in the spell's manifestation.

You will need the following:

- Solar Plexus Chakra Candle (yellow)
- Citrine crystal

- Lemon essential oil
- Matches or a lighter

To perform the spell, follow these steps:

1. Begin by lighting the solar plexus chakra candle. Place it in a safe location where it can burn uninterrupted for the duration of the spell.
2. Anoint the candle with lemon essential oil, being careful not to get any oil on your skin or clothing. This will help to activate the energy of the solar plexus chakra.
3. Hold the citrine crystal in your hand, allowing its warm energy to flow into your body. This crystal is associated with the solar plexus chakra and will help to amplify the energy of the spell.
4. Close your eyes, and take a few deep breaths to clear your mind and center yourself.
5. Repeat the following incantation:

   "By the power of the universe, I call upon the energies of the solar plexus chakra. I ask that you balance and align my self-esteem, personal power, and ability to take action. Let the energy of the citrine and the lemon essential oil guide me on my path. So mote it be."

6. Hold the citrine crystal and focus on the energy of the solar plexus chakra. Imagine a bright yellow light emanating from the area of your solar plexus, filling your body with a sense of confidence, power, and inner strength.
7. Repeat the incantation one more time, this time with even greater intention and focus.
8. When you feel that the spell is complete, blow out the candle and place the citrine crystal in a safe place.

CROWN CHAKRA BALANCING SPELL

The Crown Chakra Balancing Spell is a powerful ritual used by Wiccans to bring balance and harmony to the Crown Chakra, which is located at the top of the head and is considered the highest and most spiritual chakra. It is associated with spiritual enlightenment and higher consciousness. The spell is said to have originated in ancient India and was later adopted by Wiccan practitioners as a tool for spiritual growth and development.

The Wiccans of old believed that the crown chakra was the gateway to the divine and that it held the key to unlocking a person's whole spiritual potential. They believed that by balancing and aligning the crown chakra, one could connect with the divine and gain a deeper understanding of the universe.

As Wicca evolved and spread throughout the world, the Crown Chakra Balancing Spell became a central part of the Wiccan spiritual practice. Wiccans would gather under the light of the full moon and perform this ritual to connect with the divine and align their chakras. They would use a combination of incantations, aromatherapy, and visualization to balance and align the crown chakra.

One of the key ingredients in the Crown Chakra Balancing Spell is the use of clear quartz crystals, which are believed to enhance spiritual connections and promote clarity of thought.

The spell also often involves the burning of white candles, which symbolize purity and enlightenment.

You will need the following:

- White candle
- Clear quartz crystal
- Frankincense essential oil
- White cloth or scarf

To perform the spell, follow these steps:

1. Begin by setting up your altar, lighting the white candle, and placing the clear quartz crystal in front of it.
2. Anoint the white candle with frankincense essential oil, focusing on the energy of the Crown Chakra.
3. Sit comfortably, close your eyes, and take a few deep breaths to center yourself.
4. Hold the clear quartz crystal in your hand and repeat the following incantation:

   "By the power of the universe, I call upon the energies of the Crown Chakra. I ask that you balance and align my connection to the divine, my spiritual understanding, and my higher consciousness. Let the light of the white candle, the clarity of the clear quartz, and the purity of the frankincense guide me on my path. So mote it be."

5. Visualize a bright white light flowing into your Crown Chakra, balancing and aligning it.
6. When you feel ready, blow out the candle and wrap the clear quartz crystal in the white cloth or scarf. Please place it in a special place or carry it with you to continue the positive energies of the spell.

DREAMSCAPES AND BEYOND

SWEET DREAM SPELL

The Sweet Dream Spell has been used for centuries by Wiccans and other practitioners of magic to bring peaceful and restful sleep. Its origins can be traced back to ancient cultures that believed in the power of dreams and the role they play in our lives.

One particular story speaks of a young Wiccan woman who struggled with insomnia and frequent nightmares. She had heard of the Sweet Dream Spell and decided to try it for herself. After performing the spell, she was amazed to find that she slept peacefully and had sweet dreams every night. She shared her experience with others, and the spell soon became popular among the Wiccan community.

You will need the following:

- A pink candle
- A piece of lavender
- A piece of chamomile
- A small sachet bag
- A lighter or matches
- A pen with pink ink
- A piece of paper
- Sage or incense (optional)

To perform the spell, follow these steps:

1. Cleanse your space. Light some sage or incense and walk around your room or the area where you will be performing the spell, using it to purify the space and eliminate any negative energy.
2. Create a comfortable atmosphere. Choose a peaceful and relaxing environment to perform the spell. This could be your bedroom, a cozy corner of your living room, or even outside under the stars.
3. Gather all the ingredients in front of you.
4. Hold the piece of lavender in your dominant hand and visualize it filling with soothing energy.
5. Hold the piece of chamomile in your other hand and visualize it filling with calm, peaceful energy.
6. Light the pink candle and focus on the flame, letting your mind clear and become centered.
7. Using the pen with pink ink, write on the piece of paper your intention for the spell. You can write something like: "I call upon the powers of lavender and chamomile to bring sweet dreams and peaceful sleep."
8. Place the lavender and chamomile in the sachet bag and tie it securely with a ribbon.
9. Hold the sachet in front of you and recite the following incantation:

   "Goddess of dreams, hear my call. Bring me sweet dreams, one and all. With lavender and chamomile, I implore Bring peace to my mind and rest to my core."

10. Place the sachet under your pillow or near your bed where you will sleep.
11. Extinguish the candle and thank the goddess of dreams for her blessings.

DREAM JOURNEY SPELL

The spell was used by the witches to connect with their spiritual guides and receive messages from the divine realm. However, the spell was lost for many years after the witch trials, and it was only rediscovered by a modern-day coven of witches.

Legend has it that the coven was struggling to find a way to communicate with their ancestors and receive their guidance. One day, one of the witches had a vivid dream in which she was shown the Dream Journey Spell. She woke up with the instructions etched in her mind and shared them with her coven. They were skeptical at first, but after performing the spell, they were amazed by the clarity and power of their dream messages.

As the coven shared the spell with others, it gained popularity in the modern Wiccan community. However, not everyone was a believer, and some accused the coven of witchcraft and dark magic. The coven was forced to keep the spell a secret to protect themselves from persecution.

But the story takes a surprising turn when, many years later, the same woman who had the original dream was revealed to be a direct descendant of one of the accused witches from the Salem trials. It was then believed that the *Dream Journey Spell* had been passed down through generations of witches and was meant to be rediscovered by the modern-day coven. The spell had finally returned to its rightful owners and was no longer shrouded in mystery and secrecy.

You will need the following:

- Mugwort
- Chamomile
- Lavender
- A white candle
- A cauldron or fireproof container
- A piece of paper
- A pen

To perform the spell, follow these steps:

1. On the night of a new moon, create a sacred space for yourself, somewhere quiet and undisturbed.
2. Light the white candle and place it in the cauldron or container.
3. Take a deep breath and hold the mugwort, chamomile, and lavender in your hands, visualizing your intention of embarking on a dream journey.
4. Sprinkle a pinch of each herb onto the burning candle flame, and let the smoke rise up.
5. Place the rest of the herbs into the cauldron or fireproof container, being careful not to let the fire spread.

6. Take the piece of paper and write down a question or intention for your dream journey.
7. Hold the paper in front of the candle flame and burn it, letting the ashes fall into the cauldron or fireproof container.
8. Close your eyes, take a deep breath, and repeat the magic incantation:
   "Goddess of dreams, guide me tonight. Please show me the visions that I seek. Send me on a journey of sight, To the answers that I need."
9. Sit with the burning herbs and candle, focusing on your intention and visualizing your dream journey.
10. When you feel ready, extinguish the candle, and let the herbs continue to burn until they have burned out completely.
11. Place the ashes of the paper and herbs under your pillow, and go to sleep.

DREAM MANIFESTATION SPELL

The Dream Manifestation Spell is a powerful Wiccan spell that is said to allow you to control and shape your dreams into reality. With the right ingredients and incantations, you can harness the power of the universe to bring your deepest desires to life.

The spell was originally used by powerful witches to control their dreams and bring their desires to life. However, it was forbidden by the Church, and many practitioners of the spell were hunted down and burned at stake. Despite this, the spell was passed down from generation to generation, eventually finding its way to modern Wicca.

Legend has it that one night, a young Wiccan named Liana was unable to sleep, tormented by her unfulfilled desires. She stumbled upon an old spellbook and discovered the Dream Manifestation Spell. Desperate to bring her dreams to life, Liana performed the spell and was amazed by the results. Her dreams became a reality, and she became known as the most powerful Wiccan of her time.

However, Liana soon realized that the spell had a dark side. The more she used it, the more her dreams became twisted and corrupted. Eventually, she was consumed by her own desires and turned to the dark arts to feed her insatiable hunger for power.

Liana's story serves as a cautionary tale for those who seek to harness the power of the Dream Manifestation Spell. Use it wisely, for the consequences of your desires can be unpredictable and dangerous.

You will need the following:

- 1 dried rose petal
- 1 sprig of lavender
- 1 white candle
- 1 piece of string or ribbon
- 1 moonstone
- 1 quartz crystal
- 1 tablespoon of dried mugwort

To perform the spell, follow these steps:

1. Gather all of the ingredients together in a quiet and private space.
2. Light the white candle and place it in front of you.
3. Hold the rose petal, lavender, moonstone, and quartz crystal in your dominant hand.
4. Close your eyes and take three deep breaths, focusing on the energy of the universe flowing through you.
5. Repeat the following incantation three times:

   "By the power of the moon and the stars above, I call forth the energy of the universe with love. Let my dreams become reality. With this spell, I do decree."

6. Place the dried rose petal, lavender, and mugwort into the candle flame, allowing them to burn and release their energy.

7. Tie the string or ribbon around the moonstone and quartz crystal, creating a pendant.
8. Wear the pendant while you sleep to harness the power of the spell.

DREAM HEALING SPELL

The Dream Healing Spell is an ancient spell that dates back to the times of the ancient Egyptians. According to legend, the spell was used by the Pharaohs and their wives to protect themselves from negative dreams and to heal any nightmares that may have disturbed their sleep. The spell was passed down from generation to generation and was eventually adopted by the Wiccan community as a powerful tool for dream healing and protection.

The twist in the story is that the spell was actually created by a powerful sorceress who lived during the reign of the Pharaohs. She was known for her exceptional abilities in magic and was often called upon by the Pharaohs to help them with their most pressing problems. However, she was not satisfied with her life and longed for more power.

One day, she discovered a powerful incantation that could be used to control the dreams of others and influence their thoughts and actions. She used this incantation to create the Dream Healing Spell and offered it to the Pharaohs in exchange for greater power and influence. The Pharaohs, not realizing the true intention of the sorceress, eagerly accepted the spell and soon became addicted to it, using it every night to control their dreams and to protect themselves from nightmares.

However, the sorceress's plan was not to be realized, as the secret of the spell was eventually discovered by a group of powerful Wiccan priestesses. They were horrified by the misuse of magic and banded together to stop the sorceress and prevent the spell from falling into the wrong hands. They cast a powerful counter-spell that stripped the sorceress of her powers and banished her from the land. They then took the Dream Healing Spell and transformed it into a tool for healing and protection, and passed it down from generation to generation, ensuring that it was never misused again.

You will need the following:

- 1 White Candle
- 1 Amethyst Crystal
- 1 Sprig of lavender
- 1 Piece of rose quartz
- 1 Piece of paper and pen
- Matches or lighter

To perform the spell, follow these steps:

1. Find a quiet and peaceful space where you can perform the spell undisturbed.
2. Place the white candle in the center of your workspace and surround it with the amethyst crystal, the sprig of lavender, and the rose quartz.
3. Write down on the piece of paper any negative dreams or nightmares that have been bothering you and any other worries or fears that you want to release.

4. Light the white candle, and as you do so, close your eyes and take a deep breath. Focus your mind and concentrate on the intention of healing and release.
5. Pick up the piece of paper and hold it in both hands while repeating the following incantation three times:

"With the power of the moon and the stars above, I release these fears and these dreams that I'm done. By the power of lavender, rose quartz, and amethyst, I heal my mind and release all of this."

6. After repeating the incantation, fold the paper and place it under the white candle.
7. Focus your attention on the flame of the candle and visualize the negative energy from your dreams and worries being absorbed and burned away by the flame.
8. When you feel that the spell is complete, blow out the candle and place the amethyst, lavender, and rose quartz under your pillow.

MOONLIGHT ENCHANTMENTS

MOON DIVINATION SPELL

The Moon Divination Spell is an ancient spell that dates back to the time of the Babylonians and the Greeks. It was believed that the moon held great power and influence over human intuition and that by gazing into the moon's reflection in water or a mirror, one could connect with their innermost desires and deepest fears.

One particularly interesting story of the Moon Divination Spell involves a young witch named Hernes. Hernes was known for her strong intuition and ability to see things others couldn't, but she often struggled with the burden of her visions. One night, during a full moon, Hernes decided to perform the Moon Divination Spell in an attempt to better understand her gifts.

As she gazed into the mirror, she was suddenly transported to a dream-like state, where she was able to communicate directly with the moon. The moon spoke to her, telling her that her gift was not a curse but a blessing and that she was meant to use it to help others.

Hernes was shocked and grateful for the experience, and from that day forward, she dedicated her life to helping others through her gift. She became known as the most powerful moon diviner in all the land, and her spells and incantations

were passed down from generation to generation, eventually becoming a cornerstone of Wiccan magic.

You will need the following:

- A white candle
- A piece of moonstone or selenite
- A small mirror
- A pen and paper
- A quiet and private space
- Optional: essential oils such as lavender or jasmine to enhance intuition

To perform the spell, follow these steps:

1. Cleanse and purify your workspace and yourself, as well as any tools you will be using.
2. Cast a protective circle, calling forth the elements and any spirits or deities you feel guided to invoke.
3. Light the white candle and place it in front of the mirror.
4. Hold the moonstone or selenite in your non-dominant hand and place it on your third eye.
5. Close your eyes and focus on your breathing, imagining a white light flowing into your body and filling you with peace and calm.
6. When you feel centered and relaxed, gaze into the mirror, holding the moonstone or selenite against your third eye.
7. Repeat the following incantation:

    "Oh great moon, a reflection of the divine Shine your light on my path. Make it mine. Guide me to knowledge, truth, and clarity. Help me see the answers with grace and mercy."

8. After repeating the incantation three times, allow your gaze to soften and allow your intuition to take over. Any images, symbols, or messages that come to mind write them down on the piece of paper.
9. When you feel that you have received all the information you need, thank the moon and any spirits or deities you invoked, and close the protective circle.
10. Blow out the candle and store the moonstone or selenite in a safe place.

MOON STRESS RELIEF SPELL

Long ago, in a small village in the heart of a forest, lived a young woman named Kali. Kali was a gifted healer and often used her powers to help her village, but she was also constantly stressed and anxious. No matter what she did, she couldn't shake the feeling of unease that seemed to follow her everywhere.

One day, Kali decided to take a walk in the forest and clear her mind. As she walked, she stumbled upon an ancient circle of stones hidden deep within the forest. She had never seen anything like it before, and as she approached, she felt a strong pull toward the center.

Once in the center, Kali felt a powerful energy that filled her with peace and calm, and she knew she had found what she was looking for. She closed her eyes and meditated, and when she opened them, she saw a vision of the goddess of the moon, who spoke to her and taught her a spell for releasing stress and negativity.

Kali practiced the spell every day and noticed a drastic improvement in her mental and emotional state. She shared the spell with her village, and soon it became a popular practice for anyone who was feeling overwhelmed and stressed. Over time, the spell was passed down from generation to generation, and

the ancient circle of stones became known as the Moon Temple, a place of peace and healing for all who entered.

You will need the following:

- White candle
- Lavender essential oil
- Rose petals
- Moonstone crystal
- Matches or lighter

To perform the spell, follow these steps:

1. Cleanse yourself and your space by smudging with sage or palo santo, and set the intention of releasing stress and negativity.
2. Place the white candle in the center of your altar or workspace, and surround it with the lavender essential oil, rose petals, and moonstone crystal.
3. Light the candle and take a few deep breaths, focusing on calming and relaxing your mind and body.
4. Hold the moonstone crystal in your dominant hand, close your eyes, and repeat the following incantation three times:
5. Magic Incantation: "Goddess of the moon, hear my call, Bring calm and peace to one and all. Cleanse my mind and ease my soul, Release stress, and make me whole."
6. Visualize a bright white light surrounding you, filling you with calm and peace. See any stress or negativity leaving your body and being replaced by the light.
7. Continue to hold the moonstone crystal and repeat the incantation for as long as you feel it is necessary. When you are ready, open your eyes and blow out the candle.
8. Close the spell by saying: "So mote it be."

MOON CONFIDENCE SPELL

It is said that the Moon Confidence Spell was created by a powerful witch named Maeve, who lived during a time of great fear and uncertainty in her kingdom. Despite her own strength and powers, Maeve struggled with self-doubt and fear. One night, as she gazed upon the full moon, she was struck by its radiant beauty and felt a surge of confidence within her. Inspired by this experience, Maeve decided to create a spell that would allow others to tap into the moon's strength and confidence. She gathered the ingredients listed above and cast the spell, sharing it with her fellow witches and spreading its use throughout the kingdom. As the spell became more popular, it was discovered that the key to its success was the use of the moonstone crystal, which was said to hold the power of the moon within it. To this day, the Moon Confidence Spell continues to be used by Wiccans around the world as a way to boost their self-assurance and overcome their fears.

You will need the following:

- White candles (2)
- Moonstone crystal
- Patchouli oil
- Jasmine oil
- A piece of paper
- Pen

To perform the spell, follow these steps:

1. Choose a place where you can perform the spell where there is a clear view of the moon, preferably outside.
2. Light the two white candles and place them on either side of you.
3. Take the moonstone crystal and hold it in your hand.
4. Anoint the moonstone crystal with the patchouli oil and then with the jasmine oil while saying: "With the power of the moon and these oils, I bless this crystal with confidence and strength."
5. Write down on the piece of paper what it is that you want to feel confident about. It could be a situation, a relationship, a task, or anything that is causing you to feel uncertain.
6. Hold the moonstone crystal in one hand and the piece of paper in the other. Close your eyes and take a deep breath.
7. Repeat the following incantation three times:

   "Oh great moon, source of light and power, I call upon you in this darkest hour. Bring forth your strength, your grace, your might, And fill me with confidence day and night."

8. Fold the paper and tuck it under the candles.
9. Close the spell by saying: "So mote it be."
10. Allow the candles to burn out completely. Keep the moonstone with you as a reminder of the confidence spell.

MOON CYCLE PROTECTION SPELL

The Moon Cycle Protection Spell has its roots in ancient Wiccan traditions, where people would perform rituals and spells under the light of the moon to tap into its power. This spell was originally created by a wise Wiccan named Selena, who lived in a small village surrounded by dense forests.

One day, the villagers noticed that strange things were happening during the full moon — animals would behave erratically, crops would wither, and some people would fall ill. Concerned for the safety of the village, Selena decided to take matters into her own hands. She spent many nights under the full moon, studying its patterns and energies, and eventually discovered that the negative energies from the surrounding forest were affecting the villagers during the full moon.

Determined to protect her people, Selena crafted a spell using the powers of the moon and protective herbs, tying them together as a symbol of her intention. She performed the spell under the light of the full moon, and the results were immediate. The villagers reported feeling calmer and protected, and the negative energies seemed to be repelled.

From that day on, Selena taught the spell to the other villagers, and it was passed down from generation to generation, becoming an integral part of their Wiccan traditions. The spell became known as the Moon Cycle

Protection Spell, and it is still performed today by Wiccans around the world to protect themselves from negative energies during the moon cycle.

You will need the following:

- 1 White candle
- 1 piece of Moonstone
- 1 piece of protective herb such as lavender, rosemary, or bay leaves
- 1 piece of string or ribbon (preferably white)
- Matches or lighter

To perform the spell, follow these steps:

1. Find a quiet place to perform the spell, preferably outdoors under the moonlight or in a room with low lighting.
2. Arrange all the ingredients in front of you on a flat surface.
3. Light the white candle and hold the piece of moonstone in your dominant hand.
4. Close your eyes and take a few deep breaths, focusing on your intention to protect yourself from negative energies during the moon cycle.
5. Pick up the protective herbs and hold them in your other hand.
6. Repeat the following incantation three times, holding the herbs and moonstone tightly in your hands:

   "Under the light of the moon, I call upon the powers of protection. Shield me from harm, keep me safe and pure. As I go through this cycle, let negativity be no more."

7. Tie the herbs and moonstone together with the string or ribbon, forming a small bundle.
8. Place the bundle in front of the candle and focus on your intention for protection.
9. Repeat the incantation one more time:

   "With this spell, I seal my protection. As the moon waxes and wanes, let my safety remain."

10. Allow the candle to burn out completely, and keep the bundle with you as a talisman for protection during the moon cycle.

NEW MOON SPELL FOR NEW BEGINNINGS

The New Moon Spell for New Beginnings is a popular spell among Wiccans and has been used for centuries to help manifest new opportunities and fresh starts. This spell is typically performed during the new moon phase when the moon is in its dark phase, and the energy is focused on new beginnings and new cycles.

The spell's origin can be traced back to ancient Greece, where the goddess Artemis was associated with the moon and new beginnings. It was believed that invoking Artemis's energies during the new moon would bring good fortune and help manifest one's desires.

Over the centuries, the spell evolved and became part of the Wiccan tradition. It is now a popular spell among Wiccans who wish to bring new opportunities into their lives and start fresh in a new cycle.

One interesting twist in the history of this spell is that it was said to have been used by a powerful witch who had been wronged by a powerful king. The witch performed the New Moon Spell for New Beginnings, and her manifestation came to fruition, causing the king to fall from power and the witch to reclaim what was rightfully hers. This story serves as a reminder of the powerful energies that can be summoned

during the new moon phase and the importance of having a clear intention when performing magic.

You will need the following:

- White candles (2)
- Salt
- Sage or lavender
- A piece of paper
- A pen

To perform the spell, follow these steps:

1. Cleanse your space. Light the sage or lavender and let the smoke fill your space to purify it.
2. Cast your circle. This will help create a sacred space for your spell. You can use salt to draw the circle.
3. Light the white candles and place them on either side of the piece of paper and pen.
4. Close your eyes and take a few deep breaths. Focus your intention on new beginnings and fresh starts.
5. Write down what you would like to manifest in the new cycle. Be specific and include as much detail as possible.
6. Hold the piece of paper in your hands and repeat the following incantation: "By the light of the new moon, I call upon the energies of the universe to help me manifest my desires. May this new cycle bring new opportunities and fresh starts. So mote it be."
7. Fold the paper and place it under one of the candles.
8. Close your eyes and visualize your manifestation coming to fruition. Hold this visualization for as long as you can.
9. When you are ready, blow out the candles, thank the universe for its help, and close the circle.

RADIANT BLESSINGS

SACRED SPACE BLESSING SPELL

The Sacred Space Blessing Spell is a powerful ritual used by Wiccans to purify and consecrate a space for magical workings. It is a vital part of any Wiccan's toolkit, as it helps to create a sacred space where one can connect with the Divine and perform magic with intention and focus.

The Sacred Space Blessing Spell has been used for centuries by Wiccans as a way to create a protected and purified environment for their magical workings. The spell was passed down through generations of Wiccans, and the incantation and ingredients used have been carefully refined over time.

One particular story tells of a Wiccan named Rhiannon, who lived in a small village in the heart of the forest. Rhiannon was a powerful sorceress, and her abilities were known far and wide. However, she was also known for her humble nature and her deep love for the earth and all its creatures.

One day, Rhiannon received a vision in which she was shown the destruction of the forest and the harm that was being inflicted upon the earth. She was told that she was the chosen one to protect the earth and to use her powers for good.

Rhiannon immediately set to work, using the Sacred Space Blessing Spell to consecrate a small clearing in the heart of

the forest. She worked tirelessly, using her powers to heal the earth and protect the creatures living within it.

Years went by, and Rhiannon's powers grew stronger. She became known as the forest's protector, and her name was revered among all the creatures living within it.

However, one day, a group of hunters entered the forest, seeking to destroy all the creatures that lived within it. They reached Rhiannon's sacred clearing, intent on destroying it. But as they entered the clearing, they were met with a strange and powerful energy that filled the air.

The hunters were paralyzed, unable to move or harm the creatures within the clearing. They were filled with awe and fear, and they realized that they were in the presence of something far greater than themselves.

From that day forward, the hunters never entered the forest again, and Rhiannon's reputation as a powerful protector of the earth and its creatures only grew. The Sacred Space Blessing Spell became even more renowned as word of its power spread far and wide.

Years passed, and Rhiannon eventually passed away. But her legacy lived on, as the spell she had used to protect the forest and its creatures were passed down from generation to generation.

You will need the following:

- White candles
- Salt
- Herbs such as rosemary, lavender, and sage
- A fireproof container to hold the burning herbs
- Matches or a lighter

To perform the spell, follow these steps:

1. Clean the space you wish to consecrate thoroughly, removing any negative energy or clutter.
2. Cast a circle by walking around the perimeter of the space, visualizing a bright white light forming a protective barrier.
3. Light the white candles and place them in the four cardinal directions.
4. Sprinkle salt in each of the four cardinal directions, starting in the east and moving clockwise.
5. Light the herbs in the fireproof container and allow the smoke to fill the space, saying the following incantation:

   "Sage, rosemary, lavender, and fire, Purify this space, make it higher. With this smoke, I bless this space, And consecrate it for the work of grace."

6. Walk around the perimeter of the space once again, fanning the smoke and visualizing it, removing any negative energy and purifying the space.
7. Sit in the center of the space, close your eyes, and meditate for a few minutes, focusing on the intention to create a sacred space.
8. Open your eyes and speak the following incantation: "By the power of the elements, And the light of the Moon and Sun, I consecrate this space, As sacred and holy, so be it done, So mote it be."

CAREER BLESSING SPELL

The Career Blessing Spell is a powerful spell used by Wiccans to enhance their careers and bring success and prosperity to their professional life. It is a spell that invokes the blessings of the spirit world to help practitioner achieve their goals and overcome any obstacles in their career path.

The Career Blessing Spell has a rich history, dating back to ancient times when the Wiccan community was still in its infancy. It was passed down through generations of Wiccans, and its power was honed and refined over time.

One particular story tells of a young Wiccan named Miranda, who was struggling in her career. She was working hard, but no matter how much effort she put in, she just couldn't seem to get ahead.

Desperate for a change, Miranda decided to try the Career Blessing Spell. She gathered all the ingredients, set up her altar, and performed the spell with all her heart.

To her amazement, things started to change almost immediately. Opportunities began to present themselves, and she found herself being offered promotions and raises. Within a year, Miranda had climbed the corporate ladder and was well on her way to achieving her career goals.

However, as her success grew, Miranda began to feel a sense of emptiness. She realized that while she had achieved her career goals, she had neglected other aspects of her life, such as her relationships and her connection to the earth.

In that moment, Miranda made a decision to use her success to help others, and she dedicated her life to giving back to her community and the earth. She became known as the "Career Blessing Witch," and her name was revered among all the Wiccans who sought her guidance and advice.

And so, the Career Blessing Spell not only brought success and prosperity to Miranda's life, but it also taught her the importance of balancing success with compassion and a connection to the earth.

You will need the following:

- 1 white candle
- 1 green candle
- 1 piece of paper with your career goals written on it
- 1 pen
- A pinch of cinnamon
- A pinch of basil
- A pinch of rosemary
- A small piece of clear quartz crystal
- A bowl of water

To perform the spell, follow these steps:

1. Set up your altar with the two candles on either side of the paper with your career goals written on it. Light the white candle and then the green candle.
2. Take the cinnamon, basil, and rosemary, and sprinkle them into the bowl of water.
3. Hold the clear quartz crystal in your hands and close your eyes, focusing on your career goals. Visualize yourself achieving these goals, and imagine the spirit world guiding you toward success.
4. Begin the incantation:

   "Spirits of the universe, I call upon you to bless my career path. May your light guide me toward success and prosperity. Bless me with the strength and determination to achieve my goals. So mote it be."

5. Dip the pen into the bowl of water, and use it to write down any specific details about your career goals.
6. Repeat the incantation three times, each time with more conviction and belief in its power.
7. Once the incantation is complete, blow out the candles, and keep the piece of paper with your career goals in a safe place.

TRAVEL BLESSING SPELL

The Travel Blessing Spell is a powerful spell used by Wiccans to ensure a safe and successful journey, whether it be physical or spiritual. The spell has been passed down through generations of Wiccans and has been refined over time to include specific ingredients and incantations that work to protect the traveler on their journey.

The Travel Blessing Spell has a long and interesting history, dating back to ancient times when travelers would journey across unknown territories, facing many dangers and obstacles along the way. It was believed that by invoking the protection of the goddesses of the earth and moon, the traveler would be safe and guided on their journey.

One particular story tells of a young woman named Isadora, who was embarking on a journey to find her true purpose in life. She had heard of the Travel Blessing Spell and decided to cast it before setting out on her journey.

Isadora journeyed far and wide, facing many challenges and obstacles along the way. However, she always felt protected and guided by the spell she had cast before leaving.

One day, as she was crossing a dangerous mountain pass, a sudden blizzard hit, and she became lost and disoriented. Suddenly, she remembered the Travel Blessing Spell and recited the incantation, visualizing herself being protected and guided by the goddesses of the earth and moon.

To her amazement, the blizzard cleared, and she was able to see a path leading her to safety. From that day forward, Isadora knew that the Travel Blessing Spell was a powerful tool for anyone embarking on a journey, physical or spiritual.

The twist in the story is that Isadora never revealed the incantation of the spell to anyone else, keeping it a closely guarded secret. It was only passed down from mother to daughter within her family, and it remains a closely guarded secret to this day, known only to a select few.

You will need the following:

- A white candle
- Sage leaves
- Frankincense resin
- A piece of rose quartz
- A piece of moonstone
- A piece of amethyst
- A piece of paper and a pen

To perform the spell, follow these steps:

1. Cleanse your sacred space by smudging with sage leaves.
2. Light the white candle and place it in the center of your sacred space.
3. Burn the frankincense resin and let the smoke fill your sacred space.
4. Take the piece of rose quartz and hold it in your hand, visualizing a protective bubble of light surrounding you.
5. Take the piece of moonstone and hold it in your hand, visualizing the moon's light guiding you on your journey.
6. Take the piece of amethyst and hold it in your hand, visualizing a calm and peaceful journey.
7. Write down your destination and any specific intentions you have for your journey on the piece of paper.
8. Hold all three crystals in your hand, and recite the following incantation:

   "Goddess of the moon, guide me on my way. Bless my journey with light and safety each day Goddess of the earth, protect me from harm, And keep me safe, wrapped in your loving charm. With this spell, I now ask For blessings upon my travel task."

9. Fold the paper with your destination and intentions and place it next to the candle.
10. Let the candle burn down completely, knowing that your spell has been cast.

BLESSING OF A NEW LIFE PATH SPELL

The Blessing of a New Life Path Spell is a powerful and transformative spell used by Wiccans to help them transition into a new phase of their life and to bless their journey ahead. The spell is believed to bring guidance, clarity, and protection to those who cast it, helping them to overcome challenges and obstacles as they embark on their new life path.

The Blessing of a New Life Path Spell has been passed down through generations of Wiccans and has been used to help individuals transition into new phases of their lives for centuries.

One particularly interesting story tells of a young woman named Ophelia, who was feeling lost and uncertain about her future. She had just left a job that she didn't find fulfilling, and she was struggling to figure out what she wanted to do with her life.

One day, Ophelia stumbled upon a book of spells and incantations in an old antique shop. She flipped through the pages, and when she came to the Blessing of a New Life Path Spell, she felt an immediate pull towards it.

Ophelia gathered the ingredients and cast the spell, focusing on her desires and intentions for her future. She felt a sense

of clarity and peace wash over her as she cast the spell, and she knew that she was on the right track.

A few weeks later, Ophelia stumbled upon an opportunity to start her own business, doing what she loved most - creating art. The business took off, and Ophelia was finally on the path that she was meant to be on.

However, what she didn't know was that the spell had not only brought her clarity and guidance, but it had also brought protection and good luck. Every time she faced a challenge, she would find that a solution would present itself out of nowhere.

Years went by, and Ophelia's business became a success. She would often reflect on the Blessing of a New Life Path Spell and how it had changed her life. She became known as a successful and respected businesswoman, and she was often sought after for advice by those who were looking to transition into new phases of their lives.

You will need the following:

- A white candle
- A piece of rose quartz
- A piece of selenite
- A sprig of rosemary
- A piece of parchment paper
- A pen
- Essential oil of lavender
- Matches or a lighter

To perform the spell, follow these steps:

1. Cleanse your space by smudging with sage or palo santo or by simply taking deep breaths and visualizing any negative energy leaving your body.
2. Light the white candle and place it on a flat surface.
3. Place the rose quartz, selenite, and rosemary in front of the candle.
4. Write a description of your new life path on the piece of parchment paper.
5. Anoint the white candle with a few drops of lavender essential oil.
6. Hold the piece of parchment paper in your hands, close your eyes, and focus on your intentions for your new life path.
7. Repeat the following incantation three times:

    "Divine spirits, I call upon you. Guide me on this new path I do. With clarity, protection, and grace, Bless my journey to my new place."

8. Hold the rose quartz in your left hand and the selenite in your right hand. Close your eyes and visualize a bright, protective light surrounding you.
9. Place the piece of parchment paper under the white candle and allow it to completely burn while focusing on your intentions.
10. After the candle has burned down, take the rose quartz and selenite with you as a reminder of the blessings of the spell.

BLESSING OF THE GARDEN SPELL

The Blessing of the Garden Spell is a powerful spell used by Wiccans to bless and protect their gardens, ensuring a bountiful harvest and thriving growth.

A long time ago, in a small village nestled in the countryside, there was a wise old Wiccan named Morgen. Morgen was known for her love of nature and her exceptional abilities in Wiccan magic. She lived in a cottage surrounded by a beautiful garden that she tended to with care.

One day, the village was hit by a severe drought, and all the crops in the surrounding farms withered and died. The villagers were worried and afraid as they relied on the crops to feed their families.

Morgen, seeing the distress of her neighbors, decided to use her powers to help. She performed the Blessing of the Garden Spell in her garden, asking the powers of earth and water to bring life and abundance to the land.

The next day, the villagers were shocked to see that Morgen's garden was flourishing, with vibrant green plants and an abundance of flowers and fruits. The villagers quickly realized that Morgen had cast a spell to bless the garden, and they asked her to perform the spell in their gardens as well.

From that day forward, Morgen would perform the Blessing of the Garden Spell for the villagers, and their crops flourished, providing them with food and nourishment. As time passed, the spell was passed down from generation to generation, and it became a cherished tradition in the village.

Years went by, and the village grew, but the tradition of the Blessing of the Garden Spell remained, a testament to the power of Wiccan magic and the love of nature. To this day, Wiccans still perform the spell, blessing their gardens and asking for a bountiful harvest.

You will need the following:

- A green candle
- A sprig of rosemary
- A sprig of basil
- A sprig of lavender
- A handful of soil from the garden
- A bowl of water

To perform the spell, follow these steps:

1. Cleanse and prepare the spell area by smudging with sage or lighting incense.
2. Light the green candle and place it in the center of the spell area.
3. Take the sprigs of rosemary, basil, and lavender, and place them in a circle around the candle.
4. Hold the bowl of water in your hands and say the following incantation: "By the power of earth and water, I bless and protect this garden."

5. Sprinkle the handful of soil from the garden into the bowl of water, and say the following incantation: "May the earth and water join together to bring growth and abundance to this garden."

6. Take the bowl of blessed water and sprinkle it throughout the garden, focusing on the plants and flowers.

7. Extinguish the candle and speak these words. After that, leave the sprigs of herbs in the garden as an offering.

"Oh, powers of earth and growth, Bring life and abundance to this garden, With basil and rosemary, with lavender too, I bless this garden, make it strong and true. By the power of water, and the power of earth, May the plants grow tall and the flowers have worth. So mote it be."

BLESSING OF A NEW JOB SPELL

This spell is designed to help the caster find success and fulfillment in their new work.

The Blessing of a New Job Spell has been a staple of Wiccan magic for centuries. It is said that the earliest recorded use of this spell was by a coven of Wiccans in the 12th century. The coven was led by a powerful witch named Helga, who had a reputation for being able to cast the most powerful spells.

Helga and her coven used the Blessing of a New Job Spell to help people find fulfillment and success in their work. It was said that the spell was so powerful that even the most difficult and unattainable jobs could be obtained by those who used it.

However, there is a twist to this tale. It is said that one day, a young woman named Sarah came to Helga's coven to ask for help finding a job. Sarah had struggled for years to find work and was desperate for a solution. Helga agreed to cast the Blessing of a New Job Spell for her but warned her that the spell was not to be taken lightly.

Sarah did not heed Helga's warning and cast the spell without following the proper procedures. Instead of using the proper incantation, she simply wished for a job to come her way. And come it did. However, the job was not what she had hoped for. It was a position at a company that turned out to be corrupt and unethical, and Sarah found herself deeply unhappy in her work.

From that day on, Helga's coven began to require that those who wished to use the Blessing of a New Job Spell go through a thorough and proper process in order to ensure that they would find true success and fulfillment in their work. And to this day, the spell remains one of the most powerful and effective tools in a Wiccan's arsenal.

You will need the following:

- A green candle
- Bay leaves
- Rosemary
- Thyme
- A piece of paper
- Pen or pencil

To perform the spell, follow these steps:

1. Set up your altar in a quiet, private space where you won't be disturbed. Light some incense and take a few deep breaths to ground yourself.
2. Light the green candle and hold it in your hands. Visualize the job you want and the success you hope to achieve in this new endeavor. Focus all your energy on this image.
3. Take the bay leaves, rosemary, and thyme and mix them together in a bowl. These herbs represent success, prosperity, and good fortune.
4. Write the name of the job you want on a piece of paper. Place the paper on the altar, and sprinkle the herb mixture on top of it.
5. Hold your hands over the paper and repeat the following incantation:

   "By the power of Earth and sky, This spell will bring my job nearby. Opportunities come to me, As I will, so mote it be."

6. Visualize the success and abundance you wish to have in this job. See yourself happy, fulfilled, and prosperous.
7. When you are finished, take the paper and the herb mixture and bury them outside. As you do so, say:

   "As I bury this spell in the ground, I trust that my wishes will be found. The universe will provide. With abundance and joy, it will abide."

BLESSING OF A NEW FRIEND SPELL

The Blessing of a New Friend Spell is a powerful Wiccan magic ritual that is designed to attract a new friend into your life. This spell is perfect for those who are seeking to expand their social circle or for those who are feeling lonely and want to form a deeper connection with someone new.

Legend has it that this spell was first cast by a powerful Wiccan witch named Miranda. Miranda was known throughout the land for her kindness and generosity, and many people sought her out for advice and guidance.

One day, a young woman named Isabella came to Miranda for help. Isabella was feeling very lonely and was desperate to make new friends. Miranda knew just what to do and cast the Blessing of a New Friend Spell for Isabella.

The spell worked like a charm, and soon Isabella found herself surrounded by new friends who shared her interests and passions. Word of the spell quickly spread, and many people came to Miranda for help with the same problem.

However, as the years went by, Miranda began to worry about the power of the spell. She knew that too much of a good thing could be dangerous, and she didn't want people to become too reliant on the spell to make new friends.

So, Miranda made a bold decision. She cast a counter-spell, which would limit the power of the Blessing of a New Friend Spell. From that day forward, the spell would only work for those who truly desired friendship and were willing to put in the effort to make new friends on their own.

You will need the following:

- One pink candle
- One yellow candle
- One white candle
- A small piece of paper and pen
- A crystal or gemstone of your choice
- A bowl of salt water

To perform the spell, follow these steps:

1. Begin by setting up your altar in a quiet, peaceful location. Light the pink candle, the yellow candle, and the white candle, and place them in a triangular shape on your altar.
2. Take the piece of paper and write down the qualities that you desire in a new friend. Be specific and include both personality traits and shared interests.
3. Hold the crystal or gemstone in your hand and visualize the friend you desire. Imagine what they look like, what their personality is like, and what you will do together.
4. Place the crystal or gemstone in the bowl of salt water and let it sit for a few minutes.
5. Take the piece of paper and hold it up to the pink candle. Say the following incantation:

"By the power of the universe and the elements of Earth, Air, Fire, and Water, I call upon the energies of friendship to come to me. Bring me a friend who is true and kind, with whom I can share laughter and joy. Let the light of these candles guide the way, and let the energy of this spell go out into the world."

6. Set the paper down and focus on the candles. Visualize the energy of the spell spreading out into the world and attracting the friend you desire. Continue to meditate and focus on the candles until they burn out.
7. Once the candles have burned out, take the crystal or gemstone out of the bowl of salt water and place it on your altar. Keep it with you as a reminder of the spell you have cast.

SPELLBOUND PASSIONS

LOVE'S EMBRACE SPELL

The Love's Embrace Spell is a powerful spell that can help you attract love into your life or strengthen an existing relationship. It is a Wicca spell that has been used for centuries to help people find their soulmate or deepen their connection with their partner.

According to legend, the spell was first created by a powerful witch who had lost her lover in a tragic accident. Devastated by her loss, she spent years studying the ancient texts and practicing her craft in order to create a spell that would bring her lover back to life.

The witch traveled to a sacred site in the mountains and performed the Love's Embrace Spell under the light of the full moon. The spell worked, and her lover was resurrected, but with a twist. The resurrection caused her lover to become a vampire, and he was forced to live a life of darkness and isolation.

From that day on, the witch's Love's Embrace Spell was used with caution, as it was known to have the power to bring back lost love but also the potential to create unintended consequences.

You will need the following:

- Red candle
- Rose petals
- Lavender oil
- A small pouch or cloth bag
- Your favorite perfume

To perform the spell, follow these steps:

1. Light the red candle and place it on a table or altar.
2. Sprinkle the rose petals around the candle, making a circle.
3. Take a few drops of lavender oil and anoint the candle with it, focusing on the intention of attracting love into your life or strengthening your existing relationship.
4. Lightly spray your favorite perfume around the candle and petals, setting the intention of attracting your soulmate or deepening your connection with your partner.
5. Hold the pouch or cloth bag in your hand and imagine the love you desire flowing into it.
6. Recite the following incantation three times:

   "I call upon the powers of the universe To bring me love, to bring me joy. May my heart be filled with passion, And my soulmate comes to me with ease."

7. Hold the pouch or cloth bag close to your heart and imagine the love you desire flowing into your heart.
8. Blow out the candle, and keep the pouch or cloth bag with you at all times to attract love into your life.

WHISPERS OF LOVE SPELL

The Whispers of Love Spell is a powerful Wiccan spell that can help attract love and affection into your life.

Legend has it that the spell was first performed by a powerful witch who was deeply in love with a man who did not return her affections. The witch used her magical powers to cast the spell, and within days, the man began to show signs of love and affection toward her.

The spell was passed down from generation to generation and became one of the most sought-after love spells in the Wiccan tradition. However, it came with a twist. The spell could only be performed once in a lifetime, and if it was cast on the wrong person, it could have disastrous consequences.

It is said that a young witch once cast a spell on the wrong person, and the result was catastrophic. The man became obsessed with her and refused to let her go, causing her great harm and suffering. Since then, the Whispers of Love Spell has been approached with caution and respect, and only the most experienced and knowledgeable Wiccans attempt to perform it.

You will need the following:

- 2 Pink candles
- A piece of rose quartz
- A small jar of honey
- 1 red rose
- A small mirror
- A piece of paper
- A pen
- A red ribbon
- A small jar or container
- A drop of your own blood (optional)

To perform the spell, follow these steps:

1. Start by finding a quiet and secluded place where you can perform the spell without any interruptions.
2. Place the two pink candles on either side of the small mirror and light them.
3. Take the piece of paper and pen and write down the qualities that you desire in your partner. Be specific and detailed, as this will help the spell manifest your true desires.
4. Take the piece of rose quartz and hold it in your hand, visualizing the love and affection that you wish to attract. Imagine yourself in a loving and committed relationship surrounded by happiness and joy.
5. Take the red rose and sprinkle the petals around the candles while reciting the following magic incantation:

"By the power of the moon and stars above, Bring to me the one I truly love. Let our hearts be forever intertwined, As our love burns bright and true, divine."

6. Place the rose quartz on the piece of paper and fold it, sealing it with a drop of honey.
7. Tie the ribbon around the folded paper, making sure that it is secured.
8. Place the paper, the rose quartz, and the jar of honey inside the small container or jar.
9. Place the container or jar on the mirror in the center of the two candles.
10. Recite the following incantation:

"As I light these candles and burn this flame, I call upon the power of the universe by name. Let love and light fill my heart and soul, And guide me towards my true love, my ultimate goal."

11. Let the candles burn down completely, and keep the container or jar in a safe place.

HEART'S DESIRE LOVE SPELL

The Heart's Desire Love Spell is a powerful and ancient Wiccan spell designed to attract the love of your life. This spell works by using the power of your own heart and the natural energy of the universe to draw love to you.

Legend has it that the spell was first used by a young witch who was deeply in love with a man who did not return her affections. She consulted with the spirits and was given the Heart's Desire Love Spell as a way to draw love to herself. She cast the spell, and, to her amazement, the man of her dreams appeared at her door the very next day. They fell deeply in love and were together for the rest of their lives.

However, there is a twist to this story. As the years went by, the woman began to realize that the love she had drawn to herself was not true love. It was a shallow love based on physical attraction and surface-level qualities. She realized that true love comes from a deeper place and that the Heart's Desire Love Spell, while powerful, can only do so much. From that day forward, she dedicated her life to spreading the message that love should be based on inner qualities and true connection.

You will need the following:

- A pink candle
- A piece of rose quartz
- A piece of paper and pen
- A drop of your own blood
- A few drops of rose oil

To perform the spell, follow these steps:

1. Begin by preparing your materials and finding a quiet, peaceful space where you can focus.
2. Light the pink candle and place it on your altar or a flat surface in front of you.
3. Hold the piece of rose quartz in your hand and focus your intention on attracting love into your life.
4. Write your name and your heart's desire on the piece of paper. Fold the paper into thirds and then burn it with the flame of the candle.
5. Add a drop of your own blood to the melted wax of the candle, focusing on your intention to draw love into your life and speaking the words:

   "I call upon the power of the universe to bring love into my life. With this spell, I draw my heart's desire to me. May love find me wherever I go, and may it fill my heart with joy and happiness. So mote it be."

6. Drip a few drops of rose oil onto the candle and continue to focus on your intention.
7. Place the piece of rose quartz next to the candle and let the candle burn out completely.
8. Carry the rose quartz with you at all times to draw love to you.

LOVE'S EUPHORIA SPELL

The Love's Euphoria Spell is a powerful Wiccan spell that can create a feeling of intense love and happiness in the target of the spell. This spell is used to attract and strengthen romantic relationships and can also be used to enhance the bond between friends, family members, or even between you and your pet.

Legend has it that Love's Euphoria Spell was created by a powerful Wiccan witch named Raven, who lived in a small village in the middle ages. Raven was a young woman who was deeply in love with a man named Jack, but their love was forbidden by the village elders. Desperate to be with Jack, Raven began studying the ancient art of Wiccan magic and discovered the powerful Love's Euphoria Spell. She cast a spell on Jack, and soon he fell deeply in love with her, oblivious to the villagers' disapproval.

However, the spell had a dark side. As Jack's love for Raven grew stronger, he became more possessive and jealous, and soon Raven realized that she had made a terrible mistake. She tried to undo the spell, but it was too late. Jack had become so consumed by his love for her that he could not bear the thought of living without her. In a fit of desperation, Jack kidnaps Raven and flees the village, hoping to start a new life together.

Their love was intense, but it was also destructive. Jack's jealousy and possessiveness grew stronger each day, and Raven found herself trapped in a life that she did not want. In the end, Raven was forced to leave Jack and return to the village, heartbroken and alone.

The legend of Love's Euphoria Spell has been passed down through generations of Wiccans, a cautionary tale of the dangers of using magic to manipulate love. While the spell can create intense feelings of love and happiness, it can also lead to possessiveness, jealousy, and even obsession. Wiccans today continue to study and practice Love's Euphoria Spell, but always with caution and respect for the power of the universe.

You will need the following:

- Pink or red candle
- A piece of paper
- Pen or pencil
- A small jar
- A rose quartz crystal
- Lavender oil
- A pinch of rosemary
- A pinch of thyme
- A pinch of cinnamon
- A pinch of nutmeg
- A drop of your blood (optional)

To perform the spell, follow these steps:

1. Light the pink or red candle and sit down in a quiet and comfortable place.
2. On the piece of paper, write the name of the person you want to cast a spell on, along with any specific qualities or feelings you want to create in them.
3. Place the paper in the jar and add a rose quartz crystal to the jar.
4. Add a drop of your blood to the jar and say the following incantation:

   "By the power of the universe and the elements that surround me, I cast this spell of love's euphoria. May the feelings of love and happiness fill (name of the person) heart, and may they feel my love and my energy. May this spell bring only positivity and happiness to both (name of the person) and me. So mote it be."

5. Add a few drops of lavender oil to the jar, followed by a pinch of rosemary, thyme, cinnamon, and nutmeg.
6. Close the jar tightly and shake it gently for a few seconds.
7. Place the jar on your altar or a safe place, and let it sit there until the candle burns out.

BEWITCHING LOVE SPELL

The Bewitching Love Spell is a powerful Wiccan love spell that can help you attract the love of your life.

It was believed that by calling upon the spirits, one could align their energy with the energy of their desired partner and thus manifest their love into reality.

But as with any magic, there are consequences. Many Wiccans warned against using love spells, as they believed that true love could not be forced or manipulated. However, others argued that love spells could be used for positive purposes, such as finding a soulmate or healing a broken relationship.

Legend has it that a powerful witch named Morgana created the Bewitching Love Spell centuries ago. Morgana had lost the love of her life and was desperate to bring him back. She spent years studying the art of magic and eventually created the spell that would change her life forever.

But there was a catch. Morgana discovered that the more she used the spell, the more it corrupted her soul. She became obsessed with the power it gave her and soon found herself using it for darker purposes. Her once pure heart became consumed with darkness, and she became known as one of the most dangerous witches of her time.

It is said that Morgana's spirit still haunts those who use the Bewitching Love Spell, warning them of the consequences of manipulating love. So use the spell with caution and always remember that true love cannot be bought or forced.

You will need the following:

- A pink or red candle
- A small piece of parchment paper
- A pen
- A cauldron or fireproof container
- Rose petals
- Lavender essential oil
- A small piece of your hair
- A small piece of your partner's hair
- A drop of your blood (optional)

To perform the spell, follow these steps:

1. Begin by preparing your sacred space. Cleanse and purify the area using sage or any other cleansing method that resonates with you.
2. Light the pink or red candle and place it in front of you.
3. On the piece of parchment paper, write the name of the person you want to attract. Be specific and write down the qualities that you want in your partner.
4. Place the paper in the cauldron or fireproof container.
5. Add a few rose petals and a few drops of lavender essential oil to the cauldron.
6. Take the hair strands and your blood drop and place them on top of the paper.

7. Say the following incantation three times:

   "Love is in my heart, love is in my soul, I call upon the spirits, to make (person's name) whole. May their heart be open, may their soul be true, may they find their way to me, as I will it, so mote it be."

8. Burn the contents of the cauldron, allowing the smoke to fill the air.
9. Let the candle burn out on its own.

LOVER'S LANE LOVE SPELL

The Lover's Lane Love Spell is a powerful Wicca love spell that can help bring your true love into your life. This spell is said to have been passed down from ancient times and has been used by many Wiccans to find their soulmate.

Legend has it that this spell was created by a powerful Wiccan coven in the early days of the craft. They created the spell to help a young woman who had been searching for true love for many years. The coven members gathered together and performed the spell, and the young woman soon met her soulmate.

You will need the following:

- A red candle
- Rose petals
- A piece of paper
- A pen
- A small bottle of rose oil
- A white cloth

To perform the spell, follow these steps:

1. Begin by setting up your sacred space. Cleanse your space with a sage smudge, light some candles and incense, and meditate for a few minutes to ground yourself.
2. Take the red candle and carve your name and your intention into it using the pen. Light the candle.

3. Take the piece of paper and write down your intention. Be very specific about the qualities you want in a partner, and visualize yourself with them.

4. Sprinkle the rose petals over the paper, and then fold it three times.

5. Drip three drops of rose oil onto the paper, and then wrap it in the white cloth.

6. Hold the bundle in your hands and focus on your intention, imagining it coming to fruition.

7. Chant the following incantation three times:

   "By the light of this candle, I call to thee. Love comes to me, as I will it to be. With these rose petals, my love will bloom My true love, come to me soon."

8. Allow the candle to burn down completely, and then bury the paper and rose petals in the ground.

LOVE'S RESURGENCE SPELL

The Love's Resurgence Spell is a powerful Wiccan ritual that has been used for centuries to rekindle the love that has been lost, repair relationships that have been broken, and attract new love into one's life.

According to legend, the spell was created by a powerful witch named Rhiannon, who lived in the hills of Wales many centuries ago. Rhiannon was known for her healing abilities and was said to have used the Love's Resurgence Spell to heal broken hearts, and bring love back into people's lives.

As the story goes, Rhiannon was deeply in love with a man named Gwydion, who was a skilled warrior and a member of a rival tribe. Despite their differences, Rhiannon and Gwydion were deeply in love and planned to run away together.

However, Gwydion was betrayed by a jealous rival and killed in battle. Rhiannon was heartbroken and refused to eat or sleep, devoting all her time to mourning her lost love. One day, while wandering through the forest, Rhiannon stumbled upon a patch of herbs and flowers that she had never seen before.

As she picked the herbs, Rhiannon felt a sudden surge of energy and knew that she had discovered a powerful new magic. With the help of her fellow witches, Rhiannon crafted

the *Love's Resurgence Spell*, a potent ritual that could bring love back to those who had lost it.

The spell is quite intricate and requires several ingredients, all of which must be prepared in a precise manner.

You will need the following:

- A white candle
- A red candle
- Rose petals
- Lavender oil
- Salt
- A piece of rose quartz
- A piece of clear quartz
- A piece of amethyst
- A small bowl of water

To perform the spell, follow these steps:

1. Find a quiet, sacred space to perform the spell. Light both the white and red candles and place them on a table in front of you.
2. Sprinkle a handful of rose petals around the base of the candles.
3. Please take a few drops of lavender oil and sprinkle it on the rose petals.
4. Add a pinch of salt to the bowl of water.
5. Place the rose quartz, clear quartz, and amethyst in a triangle formation in front of the candles.
6. Sit quietly for a few moments, taking deep breaths and visualizing the love that you wish to bring into your life.
7. When you feel centered, repeat the following incantation three times:

"By the power of the moon and the stars above, I call upon the power of true love. May my heart be open and my mind be clear, So that true love may come and dispel my fear."

8. Pick up the rose quartz and hold it in your hand. Visualize the love that you desire and the happiness that it will bring to your life.

9. Place the rose quartz back on the table and pick up the clear quartz. Hold it in your hand and repeat the following incantation three times:

"By the power of the earth and the stones below, Let my heart be filled with love's warm glow. May the love that I seek come to me now, And fill my life with happiness, joy, and vow."

10. Place the clear quartz back on the table and pick up the amethyst. Hold it in your hand and visualize the love that you wish to bring into your life. Repeat the following incantation three times:

"By the power of the wind and the air above, May true love comes to me on the wings of a dove. May the love that I seek be pure and true, And bring happiness and joy that is ever so new."

11. Place the amethyst back on the table and pick up the bowl of water. Hold it in your hand and say the following incantation:

"By the power of the elements, I consecrate this water for the purpose of love and healing. May it bring me the love that I desire and heal any brokenness that I have experienced in the past."

12. Sprinkle a few drops of the consecrated water on the rose petals and repeat the incantation three times.

13. Sit quietly for a few more moments, visualizing the love that you seek coming into your life.

14. When you are ready, extinguish the candles and dispose of the rose petals in a natural setting.

SACRED PROTECTIONS

SERPENT'S PROTECTION SPELL

The Serpent's Protection Spell is a powerful ritual that can provide a shield of protection against negative energy, evil spirits, and other harmful entities. This spell is deeply rooted in Wiccan tradition and has been passed down for generations, making it a powerful tool in the hands of experienced practitioners.

According to legend, the spell was first created by a powerful Wiccan witch named Serpentine, who lived in ancient Greece. Serpentine was known for her mastery of serpent magic, and she used her skills to create a powerful shield of protection that would safeguard her from harm.

Over the centuries, the spell was passed down from one generation to the next, with each practitioner adding their own unique touches to the ritual. The Serpent's Protection Spell became one of the most powerful and sought-after spells in the Wiccan tradition, and it was often used by those who needed protection from malevolent spirits, hexes, and curses.

However, in modern times, the Serpent's Protection Spell has taken on a new meaning. Some Wiccan practitioners use it as a way to connect with the energy of the universe and to find guidance in their lives.

You will need the following:
- A black candle
- Sage
- Lavender
- Frankincense
- Patchouli oil
- A piece of paper and pen
- A serpent figurine or drawing
- A small piece of black cloth
- A piece of string

To perform the spell, follow these steps:

1. Start by cleansing your sacred space with sage to remove any negative energy that may be present.
2. Light the black candle and focus your energy on the flame, visualizing a protective shield surrounding you.
3. Take the pen and write your name on the piece of paper, followed by the words "I am protected by the Serpent's spell."
4. Anoint the candle with frankincense, lavender, and patchouli oil while repeating the incantation: "By the power of the serpent, I am protected from all harm. May the light of the universe guide and protect me."
5. Place the serpent figurine or drawing in front of the candle and wrap the piece of paper around it. Tie it together with the string.
6. Hold the bundle and recite the incantation: "Serpent of wisdom and guardian of the underworld, protect me from all that is harmful. Let no negativity penetrate this shield. So mote it be!"
7. Place the bundle on the black cloth and wrap it up. Hold it in your hands and visualize the protective shield getting stronger with each passing second.
8. Blow out the candle and bury the bundle in the ground or place it in a secret location.

GODDESS PROTECTION SPELL

The Goddess Protection Spell is a powerful Wiccan spell used to invoke the protective powers of the divine feminine. This spell can be used to protect against negative energies, harmful people, or any other negative influence in your life.

According to ancient Wiccan legends, the Goddess Protection Spell was first created by a powerful witch named Skye. Skye was known throughout the land for her incredible powers, especially her ability to communicate with the goddess herself. She created the spell in order to protect her people from invading armies and other harmful forces.

The spell quickly gained popularity among Wiccans, who began using it to protect themselves and their communities from various negative influences. However, over time, the spell's power began to wane, and it was eventually forgotten altogether.

That is until a young Wiccan named Isadora stumbled upon an old book of spells in a dusty antique shop. She was immediately drawn to the Goddess Protection Spell and decided to try it out for herself. To her amazement, the spell worked perfectly, protecting her from a dangerous situation.

You will need the following:

- A white candle
- A piece of paper
- A pen or pencil
- A small cauldron or fire-safe bowl
- A pinch of dried sage
- A pinch of dried thyme
- A pinch of dried rosemary
- A small piece of amethyst or clear quartz

To perform the spell, follow these steps:

1. Begin by finding a quiet space where you will not be disturbed. Light the white candle and place it in front of you.
2. On the piece of paper, write down the name or description of what you would like to protect yourself from. Be as specific as possible.
3. Fold the paper three times and hold it over the candle flame. As it burns, repeat the following incantation:

   "Goddess of protection, hear my plea. Keep me safe, harm none, so mote it be."

4. Drop the ashes into the cauldron or fire-safe bowl.
5. Add the dried sage, thyme, and rosemary to the ashes.
6. Hold the small piece of amethyst or clear quartz in your hand and meditate on the protective energies of the goddess.
7. Once you feel focused and centered, drop the crystal into the cauldron or fire-safe bowl on top of the ashes and herbs.
8. Light the herbs and paper with a match or lighter and allow them to burn down completely while repeating the incantation.
9. Once the fire has died down, dispose of the ashes and any remaining debris outdoors.

PROTECTION SPELL OF THE FIVE ELEMENTS

The Protection Spell of the Five Elements is a potent spell that can shield you from negative energy and protect you from harm. This spell combines the power of the five elements - earth, air, fire, water, and spirit - to create a protective shield that surrounds you.

Legend has it that the spell was first created by a powerful witch named Lyrisia. Lyrisia was known for her ability to control the elements and for her unmatched strength in battle. She was feared and respected by all who knew her.

One day, a group of hunters came to Lyrisia's village, looking for witches to burn. They had been sent by the king, who believed that witches were a threat to his power. Lyrisia knew that she had to protect her people, so she created the Protection Spell of the Five Elements.

She gathered the necessary ingredients and cast the spell, creating a powerful shield that protected her village from the hunters. The hunters were unable to see the village, and they eventually gave up and left.

After the hunters had gone, Lyrisia realized that the spell had a side effect - it had sealed the village in a bubble of protection, preventing anyone from entering or leaving. The

villagers were trapped inside, unable to go beyond the village limits.

Lyrisia was heartbroken when she realized what had happened. She had never intended to trap her people inside the village forever. But she also knew that the spell was too powerful to break and that any attempt to do so could result in the hunters finding the village.

So Lyrisia made a decision – she would use her powers to help her people thrive inside the village. She taught them how to grow crops and raise animals, and she shared her knowledge of magic with them. Together, they created a vibrant community that flourished within the protective bubble.

As time went on, the villagers forgot about the outside world, and they came to see Lyrisia as a goddess. They built a temple in her honor and worshipped her, believing that she had created a paradise just for them.

But Lyrisia knew that she was not a goddess and that her people deserved to be free. So she began to search for a way to break the spell, hoping that she could find a solution before her people were trapped forever.

Years passed, and Lyrisia grew old. She passed her knowledge of the Protection Spell of the Five Elements down to her most trusted disciples, and she charged them with the task of finding a way to break the spell.

Finally, after many years of searching, one of Lyrisia's disciples discovered a way to break the spell. But the cost was high – it required a sacrifice of great power.

Lyrisia knew what she had to do. She made the ultimate sacrifice, breaking the spell and freeing her people from the bubble of protection. But in doing so, she gave up her own life.

The villagers mourned Lyrisia's passing, but they also celebrated their newfound freedom. They honored Lyrisia as a hero, and they remembered her sacrifice for generations to come.

And so, the Protection Spell of the Five Elements became a reminder of the power of magic and the sacrifices that must sometimes be made to protect those we love.

You will need the following:

- A small bowl of salt
- A feather
- A red candle
- A small bowl of water
- A clear quartz crystal
- A white candle
- A piece of paper and a pen
- A small dish of soil
- A small dish of dried herbs (such as sage or rosemary)
- A cauldron or fireproof bowl

To perform the spell, follow these steps:

1. Begin by finding a quiet space where you can perform the spell undisturbed.
2. Cast a circle around you by sprinkling salt in a clockwise direction. As you do so, visualize a white light forming a circle of protection around you.
3. Light the red candle and hold the feather over the flame. As it burns, visualize any negative energy or harmful intentions being burned away.
4. Take the small bowl of water and hold it in your hands. Visualize the water absorbing any negative energy and purifying your spirit.
5. Hold the clear quartz crystal in your hands and infuse it with protective energy.
6. Light the white candle and place it on the piece of paper. Write down your intention to protect yourself from harm and negative energy.
7. Take the small dish of soil and hold it in your hands. Visualize the earth grounding you and providing stability.
8. Take the small dish of dried herbs and inhale the fragrance deeply. Visualize the herbs cleansing your energy and filling you with positivity.
9. Place the feather, the small bowl of water, the clear quartz crystal, the piece of paper with your intention, the dish of soil, and the dish of dried herbs into the cauldron or fireproof bowl.
10. Light the contents of the cauldron or fireproof bowl on fire. As it burns, recite the following incantation:

   "Elements of earth, air, fire, water, and spirit, I call upon your power to protect me from harm. Surround me with a shield of light and love, And banish all negative energy from my path."

11. As the flames die down, visualize a protective shield forming around you. Feel the energy of the elements surrounding and protecting you.

IRON PROTECTION SPELL

The Iron Protection Spell is a powerful spell used in Wicca magic to create a protective shield around the caster or their home. This spell is especially useful for protection against negative energy and harmful entities.

Legend has it that the Iron Protection Spell was first created by a group of blacksmiths in ancient times. They used their knowledge of metalworking to create a powerful shield of iron that could protect them from harm. They imbued their creation with magical properties, making it a potent tool for Wicca practitioners.

The spell was passed down through the generations and adapted to suit the needs of modern witches. However, a twist in the spell's history occurred when a group of hunters came to the blacksmiths' village, looking for witches to burn. The blacksmiths knew that they needed a powerful protection spell to keep themselves safe.

They came up with the Iron Protection Spell, using the iron from their forge to create a shield that could withstand even the strongest attacks. The spell worked perfectly, and the hunters were unable to harm the blacksmiths. However, the spell had an unintended side effect - it turned the blacksmiths' skin to iron. The blacksmiths were initially pleased with their newfound strength but soon realized that they were now

isolated from the rest of society. They could no longer interact with other people, and they eventually faded into obscurity.

You will need the following:

- 1 iron cauldron or bowl
- 1 iron nail
- 1 piece of paper
- A pen
- Salt
- Water

To perform the spell, follow these steps:

1. Begin by filling the iron cauldron or bowl with water and adding a pinch of salt.
2. Light a fire and place the cauldron or bowl on top of it.
3. Write your intention on the piece of paper with the pen. This could be a general statement of protection or a specific request for protection from a particular source.
4. Hold the iron nail in your dominant hand and recite the following incantation:

5. "By the power of earth and iron, I cast this spell and form a barrier. Shield me from all that would do me harm. Protect me from negative energies and entities. May this iron protection keep me safe."

6. Drop the iron nail into the water, and then drop the piece of paper into the cauldron or bowl.
7. Let the fire burn until it dies out on its own.
8. Pour the water and paper into the earth outside, thanking the elements for their protection.

FOUR CORNERS PROTECTION SPELL

The Four Corners Protection Spell is a powerful Wiccan spell that is designed to create a protective shield around a person, place, or object. This spell is often used to protect homes, businesses, and other important locations.

It is believed to have originated from a group of witches who lived in the mountains of Europe. These witches were known for their ability to communicate with the spirits of the land and the elements, and they used this spell to protect their village from invaders.

Legend has it that the village was situated at the intersection of four powerful ley lines, which made it a target for negative energies and spirits. The witches created the Four Corners Protection Spell to protect their village and their people, and it worked so well that the village remained untouched for centuries.

However, one day a group of outsiders came to the village, seeking to learn the secrets of the witches. The witches, fearing that their knowledge would be used for evil, refused to share their secrets. In response, the outsiders cast a powerful curse on the village, causing it to be engulfed in a never-ending storm.

The witches, using the Four Corners Protection Spell, were able to protect themselves and their families from the storm, but they were trapped in the village for centuries. It wasn't until a group of modern-day witches stumbled upon the village that the curse was broken, and the witches were finally able to leave.

You will need the following:

- Four white candles
- Salt
- A small bowl of water
- A feather
- A small dish of dirt or sand
- A smudge stick or incense

To perform the spell, follow these steps:

1. Start by finding a quiet and peaceful space where you can perform the spell without interruption.
2. Place the four white candles in a square formation, one in each corner of the room or area you wish to protect.
3. Sprinkle salt around the perimeter of the candles to create a circle of protection.
4. Place the bowl of water, feather, and dish of dirt or sand in the center of the circle.
5. Light the smudge stick or incense and use it to cleanse the space, starting at the north corner and moving clockwise around the circle. Repeat the following incantation as you move around the circle:

"By the power of air, fire, water, and earth, I call upon the elements to cleanse this space, And protect it from all that is harmful and negative."

6. Once you have completed the circle, stand in the center and hold your hands over the bowl of water. Visualize a white light emanating from your hands and filling the entire space. Repeat the following incantation:

"By the power of the four corners, I call upon the spirits of the earth, air, fire, and water, To protect this space and all who dwell within it, From harm and negativity."

7. Take the feather and use it to waft the smoke from the smudge stick or incense around the circle. Visualize the smoke forming a barrier of protection around the space.

8. Take a small pinch of dirt or sand from the dish and sprinkle it around the perimeter of the circle while repeating the following incantation:

"By the power of the earth, I call upon the spirits of the land and the ancestors, To protect this space and all who dwell within it, From harm and negativity."

9. Finally, extinguish the candles and give thanks to the elements and spirits for their protection.

TREE PROTECTION SPELL

The Tree Protection Spell is a powerful Wiccan magic ritual used to protect trees from harm and destruction. It is often used by those who wish to preserve the natural beauty of the world around them and to honor the life-giving properties of trees. This spell can be performed at any time of year but is most effective during the waxing moon.

Legend has it that the Tree Protection Spell was first used by a powerful Wiccan coven many centuries ago. At that time, the world was in turmoil, and forests were being destroyed at an alarming rate. The coven knew that they had to act quickly to protect the trees and preserve the natural balance of the earth.

The coven spent many days and nights in deep meditation, searching for a way to protect the trees. Finally, they came upon the Tree Protection Spell, a powerful ritual that would harness the energy of the earth to protect the trees from harm.

The coven set to work, performing the spell in the heart of the forest, surrounded by the trees they hoped to protect. They chanted the incantation, tied the green ribbon around the trees, and buried the stones in the ground.

For many years, the trees were safe, and the forest flourished. But eventually, a new threat emerged. A group of

lumberjacks arrived in the forest, intent on cutting down the trees to build a new city. The coven knew that they had to act quickly to protect the trees once again.

They returned to the forest and performed the Tree Protection Spell once more. But this time, they added a new element to the ritual. They called upon the spirits of the trees themselves, asking them to rise up and protect their own lives.

As the lumberjacks approached, they were met with an unexpected force. The trees began to sway and shake, and soon their branches reached out to the lumberjacks, grabbing their saws and axes and pulling them from their hands. The men were left standing in awe, unable to harm the trees they had come to cut down.

The coven watched from a distance, smiling in satisfaction. They knew that their spell had worked and that the trees were now protected by their own strength and power.

You will need the following:

- A piece of white cloth
- A small stone
- A green candle
- A small amount of dried sage
- A handful of fresh leaves (from any tree)
- A length of green ribbon
- A sharp knife
- A small bowl of water

To perform the spell, follow these steps:

1. Begin by finding a quiet, outdoor location where you can perform the spell without interruption. It should be a place that feels connected to nature and ideally near a tree, you wish to protect.
2. Place the white cloth on the ground and light the green candle. Sprinkle a small amount of dried sage onto the cloth, and place the stone on top of it.
3. Hold the fresh leaves in your hand and take a moment to connect with their energy. Feel their life force and their connection to the earth.
4. Using the knife, make a small cut in the skin of your finger, and squeeze a few drops of blood onto the leaves. This symbolizes your commitment to the earth and your willingness to protect it.
5. Place the leaves on top of the stone, and sprinkle a few drops of water over them. Say the following incantation:

   "Great mother of the earth and sky, I call upon your power nigh, Protect this tree from harm and plight, And keep it safe both day and night."

6. Take the length of the green ribbon and tie it around the base of the tree you wish to protect. As you do so, visualize a glowing green aura surrounding the tree, keeping it safe from any harm.
7. Return to the white cloth and extinguish the green candle. Take the stone, wrapped in the white cloth, and bury it at the base of the tree. This symbolizes your commitment to the protection of the tree.
8. Finally, take a few moments to offer thanks to the earth and the tree for their gifts. You may wish to leave an offering, such as a small amount of food or drink, as a sign of your appreciation.

GUARDIAN SPIRITS' SANCTUM

In the mystical annals of Wiccan lore, the Guardian Spirits' Sanctum emerges as a potent incantation, an enigmatic weave of ethereal energies. Crafted by ancient Wiccans to protect against the shadowy tendrils of malevolence, this spell beckons benevolent guardian spirits to enshroud the practitioner in their veiled sanctuary. The Sanctum is no mere shield; it is a binding of souls between mortal and ethereal, where mystical energies ebb and flow in harmonious cadence, and the veil between realms is drawn thin.

Legend speaks of an age obscured by darkness, where the land trembled beneath the tyranny of malevolent entities. Desperate to preserve the sanctity of the earth and their sacred traditions, the brave Wiccans embarked on a perilous pilgrimage. Through dense forests and across treacherous terrains, they sought the elusive "Sanctum of Guardian Spirits"—a secret haven rumored to house ethereal guardians, ancient beyond mortal comprehension.

Guided by celestial constellations and whispers of the wind, they reached the hidden glade at the cusp of twilight. Under the argent light of the moon, the Wiccans invoked the spirits' names with voices trembling yet resolute. An ominous silence pervaded the night until a luminous figure manifested—an ethereal guardian adorned in empyreal radiance.

The guardian spirits subjected the seekers to enigmatic trials—tests of their spirits and reverence for the natural world. Through moonlit tears, laughter, and solemn oaths, the spirits discerned the authenticity of their intentions. Finding the Wiccans worthy, the guardians granted them a fragment of their ethereal essence, binding them in a sacred covenant.

With this divine gift, the Wiccans returned to their people, bearing the Guardian Spirits' Sanctum. Unveiling the spell's power, they erected a resilient barrier against the encroaching malevolence, pledging to use it only with benevolent intent.

You will need the following:

- A quiet and secluded spot in nature, such as a forest glade, a serene meadow, or a peaceful beach.
- A small vial of water collected from a natural source like a stream or a lake.
- A handful of dried flowers or herbs that resonate with you, such as lavender, rosemary, or chamomile.
- A smooth, clear quartz crystal or any meaningful stone you find during your nature walk.

To perform the spell, follow these steps:

1. Choosing the Sacred Spot: Find a place in nature where you can sit comfortably and be undisturbed. Make sure it's a spot that resonates with you and evokes a sense of peace and tranquility.
2. Connecting with Nature: Take a few moments to ground yourself by feeling the earth beneath you and becoming aware of the sounds, scents, and sensations of the natural environment around you.

Take deep breaths and allow yourself to be present in the moment.

3. Collecting Water: If there's a nearby natural water source, such as a stream or a lake, collect a small vial of water from it. This water will symbolize the sacred connection between you and the natural world.

4. Preparing the Sacred Space: Arrange the dried flowers or herbs in front of you, creating a small arrangement that represents the beauty and abundance of nature.

5. Meditation and Visualization: Close your eyes and begin your meditation. Visualize a circle of protective light forming around you, encompassing you like a cocoon. Feel this light radiating with a sense of safety and warmth.

6. Invocation of Guardian Spirits: In your mind or aloud, express your intention to connect with the guardian spirits of nature. Ask for their protection and guidance on your journey through life with this incantation:
"Guardian spirits, ancient and wise,
By moonlit dew and starlit skies,
Stand with me in this sacred space,
A shield of protection, an enduring embrace."

7. Empowering the Symbol: Hold the clear quartz crystal or the stone you found during your nature walk in your hand. Focus your energy and intentions into it, infusing it with the purpose of protection and connection with the natural world.

8. Drinking the Water: Take a sip of the collected water, acknowledging it as a symbol of the sacred bond between you and nature. As you drink, imagine the water nourishing your body and soul, imbuing you with the spirit of nature.

9. Gratitude and Closing: Take a moment to express gratitude to the guardian spirits and the natural world for their presence and protection. Slowly open your eyes and offer thanks for the experience.

Printed in Great Britain
by Amazon

32165751R00086